THE 10 SECRETS TO HAPPINESS

Dear Jo,

It's been great working with you — thank you for your outstanding commitment, focus and all the hard work to get the Workday project back on track!

Wishing you lots of happiness & joy in your private and professional future!

Best wishes,

Alex

BASED ON THE PRINCIPLES OF THE LAW OF ATTRACTION

THE 10 SECRETS TO HAPPINESS

UNLOCK THE SECRETS TO A LIFE YOU LOVE — TODAY!

ALEXANDRA WIPF

First published in the UK in 2016 by Alexandra Wipf Ltd
(www.secrets-to-happiness.com)

Copyright © 2016 Alexandra Wipf Ltd

All rights reserved. No part of this publication may be reproduced, distributed or transmitted in any form or by any means, including photocopying, recording, or other electronic or mechanical methods, without the prior written permission of the publisher, except in the case of brief quotations embodied in critical reviews and certain other non-commercial uses permitted by copyright law. For permission requests, contact the publisher, Alexandra Wipf Ltd, through the website shown above.

All quotes and references to the teachings of Abraham are copyrighted material © Esther Hicks, www.abraham-hicks.com, and used with permission from Esther Hicks.

ISBN: 978-0-9956753-1-5

Because everyone deserves to be happy

CONTENTS

Introduction 1

PART 1: A FEW KEY UNDERLYING PRINCIPLES

The Law of Attraction – you create your own reality 11

Happiness is a choice 25

The power of the underlying belief system 33

PART 2: THE 10 SECRETS TO HAPPINESS

1st Secret: Choose what is 49

2nd Secret: Be in the moment 65

3rd Secret: Stop worrying, feeling guilt and regret 75

4th Secret: Get off it 85

5th Secret: Give your life a purpose 97

6th Secret: Be intentional 109

7th Secret: Do it now 117

8th Secret: Simplify your life 127

9th Secret: Nurture your body, mind and soul 141

10th Secret: Appreciate what you have 161

And now: over to you! 173

Acknowledgements 183
Glossary 185
Further reading 189
References and sources 191

INTRODUCTION

Welcome to your adventure called life!

This is it. The beginning of an exciting journey to a happier life. Are you ready?

Life is meant to be a joyful adventure, and you were born to thrive. For many, however, life has turned into more of a struggle than a fun experience. It seems that when we grow up, we lose the light-heartedness of our early years, and everything becomes increasingly serious and hard work. We beat ourselves up about the mistakes we make along the way, and get disenchanted about life. Its magic and miracles, which captivated us as children, are filed away as 'figments of our imagination'. It's official: we have become responsible, sensible adults. Let's leave having fun to the little ones; we've got work to do!

But it doesn't have to be this way. It's time to rediscover what life is really about, and find our way back to a happier and more playful way of being. If we could only remember how excited we were to live this life before we were born! Did you know that you are exactly who you wanted to be, with all your (perceived) flaws and imperfections? Before you were born, you chose to be you, out of billions of options. Your soul was ready for a thrilling adventure, and excited about all the challenges that you were going to be faced with throughout your life. You knew that each and every one of them was going to be an opportunity to grow and to explore what's possible.

Now, you might completely disagree with the above statement. How could you have possibly chosen this life, where nothing ever seems to work out as you would like it to? No matter whether your life is pretty good already, or about as bad as it can get – I invite you to be open minded while you read this book. Try the ideas and techniques presented, and find out what difference they could make in your life. Because here's the thing: when you change the way you look at things, the things you look at change. And I'm not just making this up – this is a very powerful and simple coaching technique called reframing. So give it a go – your happiness might depend on it!

We all want to be happy

Have you ever met anyone who doesn't want to be happy? Neither have I. Yes, we might strive for very different things. But whatever it is that we want, we usually go after it because we believe it will make us happy. We might be aiming for a fulfilling relationship, a happy family, a healthy and slim body, a better career, more money, fame, a fancy car, a big house, or all of these things – the list is unique to each individual. No matter what it is we strive for, though, the underlying motivation is the desire to be happy.

So we work very hard to get the things we think we need to make us happy. The problem is, once we finally have what we always wanted, after years of sweat and tears, we realise that the newfound happiness is often short lived. All of a sudden there is something else we need as well, in order to be completely happy. And here is why: because we will never get there. 'There' being the ultimate destination where happiness rules, day in and day out, because we finally have everything we ever wanted. In reality, happiness is something that is recreated anew, every single day.

Happiness doesn't exist as a destination; it's all about the journey. Or, as Christopher Plummer put it in the movie *Hector and the Search for Happiness*, "We should concern ourselves not so much with the pursuit of happiness, but more with the happiness of the pursuit." All happy people have one important thing in common: a willingness to continuously create a feeling of joy every single day, no matter what the circumstances. This book will show you how to do that.

Things that prevent us from being happy

Do you know what stops you from being happy? What story are you telling yourself that explains why you are not as happy as you could be, right now? There are many things that can keep us from being happy, but from general observation and working with coaching clients over the years, I have noticed that some are more common than others. As awareness is always the first step to taking control of your life, it is worth being mindful of the following two 'misery traps':

- **It is normal to not be happy, isn't it?** In modern society, many of us have become cynical and resigned about what is possible regarding happiness. We accept a life of mediocrity, of contentment, rather than outrageous joy. Even as I am writing this, I am wondering if asking for 'outrageous joy' is asking for too much. Yet it really isn't! We simply believe it is normal to not be happy – and we set our expectations accordingly. Living a truly fulfilling and happy life is not usually a day-to-day occurrence, so we draw the conclusion that happiness must be difficult to find.

- **Dependence on external circumstances.** This is a big one, a myth that is keeping many people from living a happier life: we think that happiness is caused by external circumstances, and that we can only be happy if our surroundings present themselves in a certain way. We might blame our unhappy state on a shortage of money, a difficult relationship, a lack of a partner, a boring job, or the weather – whatever the reason, it is always something or someone else's fault that we are not as happy as we could be. Since we are normally unable to influence our environment sufficiently to make it perfect for us, true happiness becomes a fragile and rather rare occurrence. In other words, the belief that our happiness is not in our control means we often end up dissatisfied and unhappy. But happiness is a state of mind and comes from within, and is only driven by circumstances as much as we allow them to influence us.

> **Exercise**
>
> Think about what is stopping you from living a fulfilling and happy life, right now. Does it fit into either of the two categories above? Or is it something else? Whatever the reason – become fully aware of it and acknowledge it, as awareness is the first step to a breakthrough in creating a joyful life you love.

The biggest secret of them all

What if I told you that your dreams could come true, but the price you have to pay is happiness? In other words, learn to be happy, and your dreams will come true. Not too much of a sacrifice, is it! That is exactly what this book is about. Because here is the biggest secret of them all, the secret that triggered the writing of this book: whatever you think is missing in your life to be completely happy, you have to be happy first before it can come into your life. Sounds paradoxical? Absolutely. Throw the notion of 'you have to see it to believe it' out of the window. To make this work, you have to 'believe it to see it'! So for example, if you are single and looking for the love of your life, get happy and he or she will come into your life. If you think you are overweight and every diet you have tried has failed, get happy and the pounds will start to drop off, easily and naturally. If you want more money to buy a bigger house or go on an extended holiday, get happy and the money will come into your life in miraculous ways.

Why is that? It all comes down to the Law of Attraction, which I will explain in more detail in the next chapter. For now, let's just say that happiness cleans up the signals you send to the Universe about your dreams and desires, and gets rid of all the resistance or 'white noise' that stops you from bringing what you want into your life. The purpose of this book is to show you the secrets to achieving happiness no matter what your circumstances, so that you can manifest into your life what you have always wanted. In other words, this book will not only provide guidance on how to remove the obstacles to happiness, it will also help you to make your dreams a reality, whatever they may be. Now that's what I call a great '2 for 1' deal!

How to use this book

Imagine if there was just one thing in this book, just one idea, exercise, tip or method that would make you a happier person, permanently. Wouldn't that one thing alone make it worth reading this book? And of course there is much more than that. In fact, the following chapters encapsulate the essence of everything I have discovered over many years of research and hands-on application of the Secrets to Happiness. As a successful personal and executive coach I have worked with many people and have explored a wide range of philosophies, tools and methods. I have faced my own personal difficulties, particularly in the areas of relationships and health, and have travelled extensively around the world, looking for answers. I have explored Kabbalah, Ho'oponopono, and 'A Course in Miracles', to mention just a few philosophies, and have experimented with hypnosis, rebirthing, past life regression, out-of-body experiences, and many forms of meditation (the glossary provides more detail on these various techniques and philosophies). I have subjected myself to countless seminars and coaching training courses, and have of course read many, many books. I have met gurus and spiritual healers on my journey, and have experienced many highs and lows along the way. The following chapters summarise my key findings about the Secrets to Happiness, complemented with interesting, real-life examples and simple exercises to help you start creating a life full of joy.

The structure of the book is simple: Part 1 contains some key underlying principles to set the foundation for a happy and rewarding life; Part 2 explains the 10 Secrets to Happiness. Together, the two sections provide a powerful manual for the game of life, and a comprehensive guide to start living a life you love – today! Since we are all different, I will not claim that all 10 Secrets to Happiness will speak to you in the same way. Chances are, there will be a few secrets that you are mastering well already, without even realising it. Then there may be a couple that really push your boundaries, taking you out of your comfort zone. I suggest spending at least one day per chapter, applying that specific secret to everything you do – make it your mantra for the day, so to speak. Explore what difference the suggestions in the chapter can make in your life. The exercises that complement each chapter will provide support in translating the content into your own life, and will make it real for you. Bearing in mind we all have busy lives, I have deliberately kept the number of exercises to a minimum, choosing only the most impactful – the ones that will make the biggest difference. Once you have experimented with each secret, I suggest picking the one, two or three at most that have made the biggest difference to you, and embedding them in your life as new habits. The closing chapter will show you how to do so.

But enough said. Let the adventure begin!

PART 1:
A FEW KEY UNDERLYING PRINCIPLES

Are you aware of your underlying world view, your answer to why you are here and how it all works? Did you know that you have a choice about what this underlying world view looks like, and that if it doesn't provide you with a positive, supporting context, you can choose again? I invite you to read the next three chapters with an open mind, try the ideas and principles presented, and see what a difference they can make in your life.

THE LAW OF ATTRACTION – YOU CREATE YOUR OWN REALITY

You are meant to live an expansive, exhilarating, good-feeling experience. It was your plan when you made the decision to become focused in your physical body in this time–space reality. You were born knowing that you are a powerful Being; that you are good; that you are the creator of your experience, and that the Law of Attraction (the essence of that which is like unto itself is drawn) is the basis of the Universe, and you knew it would serve you well. And so it has.

Abraham (channelled by Esther Hicks)[1]

Introduction

The Law of Attraction has been a popular subject ever since the movie and the book *The Secret* were released in 2006. Since then many books have been written about the Law of Attraction, yet a lot of people still seem to struggle to realise their dreams. It turns out that putting the theory into practice is harder than it seems. Of all the books and other materials I have studied over the years on this subject, I find the teachings of Abraham the most practical and impactful. The following chapter – with the exception of the scientific context provided at the start – is therefore based on these teachings.[2] It takes the essence of the key concepts of the Law of Attraction as explained by Abraham, summarised in my own words and specifically focused on the areas that, from my own observations and experience over the years, are the most challenging to apply.

Abraham's teachings have had – and continue to have – a profound and lasting impact on my life. They have laid a solid foundation for the happy and fulfilling life I am living today, and work incredibly well in conjunction with the 10 Secrets to Happiness. Several of the 10 Secrets have a direct link to the Law of Attraction, so this chapter is merely an introduction to the basics of the Law of Attraction, which will be put into a more specific context in Part 2 of the book.

Abraham is a group of non-physical entities that has been channelled by Esther Hicks since 1985, and has a large following, particularly in the United States. If you would like to learn more about the Law of Attraction and the teachings of Abraham, take a look at their website, www.abraham-hicks.com. Many of their video clips are available for free on YouTube.

Scientific context

The Law of Attraction is still largely unexplained from a scientific perspective. However, there are a few ideas that can be linked back to science, and quantum physics in particular. In the year 1905, Albert Einstein proved that there is a direct relationship between energy and matter, with his famous formula $E = mc^2$ (energy equals mass multiplied by the speed of light squared). So we now know that when we break matter down into the smallest subatomic particles, we move beyond the material realm and into a realm in which everything is energy. Experiments have also shown that at the subatomic level (at the level of protons, neutrons, electrons and even smaller particles), nothing stands still – everything moves, everything vibrates. Solid matter vibrates at a lower frequency, while other energy forms like air vibrate at a higher frequency.

As such, it is a scientific fact and now the basis for quantum physics that we live in a Universe that is built on energy and vibration.

There have also been some scientific studies that suggest that the outcome of experiments with subatomic particles is not completely independent of the observer's expectation. In other words, the expectation of the observer seemed to influence the behaviour of the subatomic particles. It is then not such a huge leap of faith anymore to consider the notion that, at a very core and fundamental level, the Universe and its particles might be influenced by human intention and expectation, which is where the Law of Attraction comes in.

What is the Law of Attraction?

The Law of Attraction provides us with an explanation of how the Universe works in our day-to-day environment. Just as our bodies represent energy and vibration, so do our thoughts. And since thoughts are simply a higher frequency version of matter, they are the first step to manifestation. The Law of Attraction states that we attract the essence of what we think about the most, and what we give most of our attention and emotional energy to. Or in other words, if you think about something long enough, it will eventually become a reality.

The Law of Attraction is like the Law of Gravity. It is there whether you know about it or not, and it works in the same way for everyone, day in and day out. Gravity doesn't just apply sometimes; as long as you are on Planet Earth, gravity will keep you on the ground, and you can fully rely on that fact. It works in exactly the same way for the Law of Attraction. It doesn't just work for the people that know about it; it applies equally to all 7 billion human beings on this planet. However, knowing about the Law of Attraction, and understanding how it works and how to apply it, means you can be a much more proactive player in the game called life, and create a happier and more fulfilled life for yourself.

Applying the Law of Attraction

So, the underlying idea of the Law of Attraction is simple: you attract what you think about the most. And it works consistently, every single time. So why is it then that so many people that know about the Law of Attraction don't seem to be able to attract what they want into their lives?

Applying the Law of Attraction consists of three steps:

Step 1: Be clear about what you want
Step 2: The Universe hears what you want and responds to it
Step 3: You allow the Universe to get it to you

Step 2 happens without your intervention, but there are two fundamental challenges involved with Steps 1 and 3 which can slow down the desired manifestations significantly:

- **Being absolutely clear what you want**: Having coached many people over the years, most are quite clear that what they currently have is not what they want. However, when asked to put into words and pictures specifically what it is exactly that they do want, many people only have a vague notion and – even worse – a continuously changing idea of what they want.

- **Focusing on what you want, rather than what you don't want**: We live in an attraction-based Universe, which means it doesn't matter whether you say "Yes I want this" to something, or "No I don't want that". As soon as you give it your attention, you will start to pull it towards you. So the more you notice and focus on things you don't want, the more you will attract them into your life. The key is to learn to not get absorbed by the things you don't like. Instead, shift the focus to getting excited about what it is you do want, and you will start to see the Law of Attraction bring it to you in no time.

We will now explore both of these challenges in more detail, and I will share with you some of my favourite tools and techniques to make the Law of Attraction work for you.

Get clarity about what you want

In my capacity as a coach, the first thing I do with a new coaching client is to establish what the client would like to get out of the coaching, as well as get clarity on their bigger life goals in general. Many people I work with are not very clear about what they are looking for in life, and what true happiness looks like for them. And speaking to people from all walks of life over the years, I have come to the conclusion that this is not a phenomenon for coaching clients alone. Some might have a general idea of what it is they are looking for, like 'I want to lose weight', 'I want to be healthy', 'I want to find a partner', 'I want to have a family and children', or 'I want a bigger house and a nicer car'. But when asked for more detail, why they deserve to have that better paying job, what it would feel like to have that bigger house, or where they see themselves in five years' time, many draw a blank. Do you know what you want, and why you deserve it? Do you have a clear picture in your mind of your hopes and dreams?

To make the Law of Attraction work for you, I always suggest using visualisation to get excited about the detail of what it is you want and what your future will look like. Vision boards are one of my favourite tools, which are simply a large sheet of paper (ideally size A0 or A1) where you paste any pictures and words that inspire you and represent what you would like to experience. Make sure you have fun with this – the process of creating the vision board, and getting excited about what you put on it, is a key part to making your dreams a reality. Then frame the finished piece and look at it often, as a daily reminder to get you into a place of positive anticipation about what is coming into your life. It is important, though, not to get too attached to any specific detail (that specific house, that specific partner), as this limits the Universe's creativity and scope to bring you something even better. Instead, focus on the general feeling of happiness and excitement for what is coming, and how it will make you feel when you get there, and allow the Universe to do the rest.

I created my first vision board back in 2008, and the main themes on it were travel, finding my soulmate, and starting a family. And even though I was a long-term singleton approaching my mid-thirties at the time, all of these things have since become a reality. The new vision board which my partner and I made in 2014 is an important feature in our living room, and we look at it often. One of the main elements on it, to build our very own dream house, started to manifest a lot quicker than we ever expected, after the right opportunity presented itself for us to buy a piece of land. A vision board that excites you when you look at it will keep you focused and remind you (and the Universe) of your priorities, and send opportunities your way. If you haven't got one yet, get it started this week!

Exercise

Do you know what you want in the areas of relationships, health and body, money, work and career, home, or any other area that is important to you? Pick the one area you are most passionate about seeing a change in, and flesh out in detail what you are looking for. What will it feel like when you have it? Combine your list with a vision board as described, and have fun with the process of creating a clear picture of your desired future.

Once you are absolutely clear about the 'what', spend some time on the 'why': Why do you want this? Why do you deserve to get it? The reason why you want something defines the essence of what it is that you want. Only if you believe that you are worthy of getting what you desire can the Universe actually bring it to you, because if you don't believe you can have it, that vibration will keep it away.

Important note: Your job is to focus on the 'what you want' and 'why you want it'. The 'how' and 'when' is the Universe's job. As soon as you start to focus on the 'how', you will bring doubt and resistance into the process, which will keep your manifestation at bay. So just focus on the fun parts with the 'what' and 'why', and leave the rest to the infinite creativity of the Universe to figure out.

Learn to focus on what you want rather than what you don't want

It doesn't sound difficult, but focusing on what you want rather than what you don't want is very challenging, and is probably the biggest reason why so many people struggle to make the Law of Attraction work for them. Why is that? Typically, you will focus most of your attention on your current environment, on 'what is' – what you see, hear, smell and taste, right now. And the clearer you are about what it is you want, the more you will notice how your current reality doesn't yet reflect that. Which means that, naturally, your focus is on the lack of what you want, on not having it yet. So for example, if you would like more money, you are bound to be reminded of your lack of money every time you see something you would like to buy but can't. This disappointment (or in other words, this focus on what you don't want) will prevent more money from coming into your life.

Example

Weight loss is an area where people often get stuck focusing on what they don't want (the extra weight), which is what makes it so difficult to lose the weight. It's almost like the extra weight clings to people that have an issue with their weight, while others lose pounds easily when they need to – simply because they don't think about it much. People struggling with their weight bring all sorts of negative emotions to the conversation. By focusing on the extra pounds, seeing themselves in the mirror, standing on the scales every day, and following a tough weight loss regime, they continuously focus on the 'what is' (i.e. the extra weight) and therefore reinforce what they don't want.

If you are unhappy about your weight, the best way to lose the extra pounds is to stop focusing on the scales and any food deprivation, and instead focus on what you do want – such as experiencing more energy and feeling healthier. Focus on the positive emotions that come with those visualisations, and combine them with healthy food and some gentle exercise you enjoy. Using positive affirmations is another very powerful tool to get into a positive frame of mind, which we will look at in the chapter 'The power of the underlying belief system'. Ultimately, it's about finding a place of happiness no matter how many extra pounds you think you have. Stop thinking about it! Instead, focus on feeling full of energy. And then, after a few months of healthy food, gentle exercise and positive thoughts, when you have long forgotten that you ever had an issue with your weight, you suddenly realise that you can fit into your favourite jeans again.

Make the Law of Attraction work for you: the role of emotions

Let's recap. Your thoughts are the basis for your manifestations – whatever you think about the most will come into your life. It would therefore make sense to try to manage individual thoughts by focusing on specific things. However, on average, people think over 50,000 thoughts a day. Trying to monitor your thoughts is therefore a futile exercise – your brain is simply too active to keep your thoughts in check. On the other hand, it is quite easy to pay attention to your emotions. Emotions provide the underlying theme to your thoughts, and play a key role in your manifestation power. While your thoughts might change second by second, the underlying emotion is likely to stay the same for much longer. And the stronger the emotion, the more actively you are participating in the process of manifestation.

Do you know whether you are currently attracting what you want, or pushing it away? With your emotions, you have a very simple and powerful guidance system to hand: if you feel positive emotions, such as joy, enthusiasm, passion and appreciation, you are creating more of what you want in your life. On the other hand, if you are experiencing negative emotions, such as anger, jealousy, frustration, or disappointment, you are focused on what you don't yet have, and these negative emotions are pushing the things you want away.

So all you ever need to do as a powerful, deliberate creator who understands the Law of Attraction is to tune in to your emotional guidance system, and focus on any thoughts that make you feel good. That's it! Make it your priority to get happy, which allows the Universe to bring you what you want. If you find it difficult to find anything positive to focus on in a certain situation, it is a good idea to step away from that environment – even just for a few minutes – and instead focus on something that will make you feel better. Also, start to notice when 'but' creeps into your language and your thinking, as it's an excellent indicator that you are focusing too much on the lack of what you want, and the impossibility that you associate with getting it.

Example: how I found my soulmate

Romantic relationships are a very emotional subject by nature, and an area where people often focus on what they don't want. Those that are in a relationship might focus on the traits of their partner they don't like, while people that are single might think a lot about not having found the right partner yet, feeling lonely as a result. I have learned this lesson very painfully, and it took me over a decade of being single before I finally got the message. So let me tell you my story of how I found my soulmate.

I was mostly single until my mid-thirties, with just a few interludes of short relationships. I was very clear in terms of what I wanted (a loving relationship), but I was so focused on the fact that I didn't have it yet, that nothing seemed to work. I tried many different things over the years, including internet dating, speed dating, single social events, various Meetup groups and Ceroc dancing, amongst other things. I even went to rugby games, telling myself I was just going because of the game, not because of the (mostly male) spectators... But even though I met great people along the way, that loving relationship I was craving so much remained out of my reach. I came to the conclusion that something was obviously wrong with me, that I was simply unable to be in a relationship, so went through a bout of relationship seminars and even more exotic things like rebirthing and hypnosis, but that didn't make any difference either – until I realised that I was going about it completely the wrong way. I was so focused on 'fixing' my situation and myself, that all my attention was continuously centred on the lack of a relationship. When I learned about the Law of Attraction, I realised that I was in the wrong frame of mind to meet my soulmate. I felt lonely and sorry for myself. I was so far away from feeling happy, how could I possibly attract a happy relationship? I had to find a place of happiness first, and then the relationship would come, not the other way round!

Of course that is much easier said than done. How do you get happy, when the one thing you think you need the most to be happy is missing in your life? So I decided to take some rather drastic action. I took a three-month timeout from work, and went to New Zealand. I travelled for a few weeks to explore the beauty of this stunning country, and then spent seven weeks on my own in a cute little house by the beach. I listened to uplifting Law of Attraction materials from Abraham every single day, and just focused my days on feeling fantastic (rather than lonely). I went for long walks along the beach, read about forty books (I love reading, so yes, I really did), explored the area and just luxuriated in the knowing – really, truly knowing – that I was about to meet my soulmate. I let go of trying to force meeting someone, and just enjoyed spending time on my own and getting truly happy. Those seven weeks were some of the best weeks of my life and were worth every penny: four months later, I met my soulmate – after being single for over fifteen years! We got engaged eighteen months later, and are now living as a happy little family with our beautiful young daughter. So by spending seven weeks on Step 3 of the Law of Attraction ('allowing the Universe to get it to you'), I brought into my life a gorgeous man and my own family, things that had eluded me for a very long time.

Now just to be clear, I'm not suggesting that you quit your job and emigrate to New Zealand to find your place of joy and happiness. Just find a way to distract yourself from what is bothering you in your life or environment, and find a way to be happy – for example, by reading the remainder of this book! Once you are happy and feel excitement and positive anticipation rather than disappointment, what you desire will come into your life. You will know that you are very close to manifesting what you want when you no longer feel disappointed because you don't have it yet, but instead feel a sense of excitement and certainty that it is coming. At that point your vibration is aligned with your desired end state, and you are in a place where you can receive what you have been asking for.

Implications of the Law of Attraction

Understanding and accepting the Law of Attraction as the rule of the game has quite fundamental consequences. It means that you can no longer blame outside circumstances for your situation – you are the creator of your life and your reality. This is sometimes difficult to see because of the time lag between your thoughts and the manifestation, but it means you have a lot more power than you might realise. When you take full accountability and observe what is happening around you, you will start to see a link between your predominant thought patterns and what is occurring around you. For example, if you are experiencing a very stressful and frustrating work environment, consider that it might be reinforced, or even created, by your focus on stressed out and frustrated thoughts and emotions. The stronger you feel about something, the more you are an active creator of your environment.

Once you start to see the Law of Attraction at play, you will start to understand that the Universe wants you to win and live a happy and fulfilling life. You will start to see the beauty of how the Universe works its magic to bring to you – in very often completely unexpected ways – what you want. Opportunities are endless, and it's time to make the most of the amazing adventures that life has to offer.

Just to clear up a common misconception from the start, though: once you 'get there', and have realised your desires, it won't be the end of your journey. Whether it's your dream house, your dream job or your dream partner – there will be many things about your manifestation that you love, but as you are experiencing that new situation you will discover things about it that you would like to experience differently. So from that new viewpoint you will desire new things, and your creative process of manifestation continues. This is what life is all about, sifting through what you want and what you don't want to get absolutely clear about what you desire, and then enjoying the process of making your dreams a reality while continuously evolving and growing and identifying new and even bigger dreams.

Closing note

There is a very strong link between the focus of this book – the Secrets to Happiness – and the Law of Attraction. The most important ingredient required to realise your desires is to get happy. Very often, we get sidetracked by trying too hard, and if our dreams don't become a reality quickly enough, we get frustrated – which keeps the manifestations away.

I would therefore recommend the following: now that you know how the Law of Attraction works, get clear on what it is that you want to bring into your life, and then put the remaining knowledge of the Law of Attraction aside for the time being. Read the remainder of this book instead and practise the 10 Secrets to Happiness, and see which ones work best for you. By rediscovering what it feels like to experience happiness every single day, and making 'feeling good' a priority in your busy schedule, you are naturally doing everything you need to do in order to manifest your desires. This is literally the only thing you need to remember: there is nothing more important than that you find a place of happiness. The better you feel, the stronger the lever of attraction to bring what you desire into your life.

You will start to see it with the little things first – everything will seem to become easier, with more and more things just falling into place as if by magic. What seem like lucky coincidences will become regular occurrences. And then it won't be long before your bigger dreams start to become a reality, leading you to take inspired action to make things happen. Just don't forget, having an enjoyable journey is key, so don't get too heavy and serious about it. Or as Abraham put it: "You're always, always, always going to be on your way to something more – always. And when you relax and accept that, and stop beating up on yourself for not being someplace that you're not, and instead, start embracing where you are while you keep your eye on where you're going – now life becomes really, really, really fun."[3]

HAPPINESS IS A CHOICE

I, not events, have the power to make me happy or unhappy today.
I can choose which it shall be.
Yesterday is dead, tomorrow hasn't arrived yet.
I have just one day, today, and I'm going to be happy in it.

Groucho Marx (American comedian, 1890–1977)

How circumstances rule your life – and your happiness

Life is full of challenges. And no doubt full of reasons why you aren't as happy as you could be. Do you know what needs to change in your life for you to be completely happy? Are there people in your life who don't behave the way they ought to? Are you short on money, need a bigger house, or more sleep? Or perhaps you don't enjoy your job, are unhappy about your body and looks, or have an issue with your health? Most of us have at least one – if not several – perfectly reasonable explanations why we aren't as happy as we'd like to be. And whatever the reason, most of us think we can only be happy once these circumstances change for the better.

But as the previous chapter explained, you are a powerful creator. You create your own reality, which means you are also in charge of your happiness. Happiness is a state of mind, and therefore only determined by external circumstances as far as you allow them to influence you. You can have everything in the world and still be miserable. Or you can have very little and feel very joyful. Happiness can be experienced under even the most difficult situations, and is a choice you can make at any point in time. Your happiness is your right and your responsibility, and therefore under your control – don't let your circumstances rule your life. You are in the driving seat of your happiness!

> **Exercise**
>
> If you haven't done so already, make a list of the things that currently stop you from being happy, right now. What are the reasons that keep you from living an outrageously happy life? Keep these in mind when reading Part 2 of the book. Secrets 1 and 4 in particular will help to transcend those limiting reasons.

Don't expect others to make you happy

Here is an important fact: the people in your life are not responsible for your happiness. Wait, what? Isn't the most important role of the other person in a relationship – particularly a romantic relationship – to make you happy? No, actually it isn't. If you expect your partner to make you happy, by being a certain way or doing certain things, it puts a lot of strain on the relationship. The other person will consciously or subconsciously feel pressured to live up to those expectations, and will eventually become resentful of the situation. Or, if your partner doesn't live up to your expectations, it will be you who becomes resentful and disillusioned at some point. Either way, it is not the answer to a happy and fulfilling long-term relationship. It is much healthier and more balanced if both people in the relationship take responsibility for their own happiness.

But what about 'soulmates'? Will your soulmate, that elusive perfect partner who's out there somewhere, not ensure your happiness? A lot of people spend years looking for the perfect relationship and the perfect partner. I mentioned in the previous chapter that I was one of them, too. So let's clear up one common misconception about soulmates: finding your soulmate does not mean that you won't have any more arguments in a relationship. Yes, your soulmate will ignite that 'special spark' in you, and be a great match. But not even soulmates are perfect, and just like anyone else they will have some flaws and annoying little habits – because last time I checked, soulmates were all human, too! So even if you find your perfect match, it's important not to expect him or her to ensure your happiness.

When I met my soulmate after many years of searching, I was completely happy with myself – before I met him. I had finally fallen in love with myself and my life, and was ready to be with someone. I no longer expected my partner to be in charge of my happiness, to be that 'missing piece of the puzzle' I couldn't live without. Can you imagine what pressure that took off him and the relationship? I just wanted him to be himself, and it made all the difference. Because I'm pretty sure even though I was finally with my soulmate, without finding my own place of happiness first it would have just been another short-term relationship. So find a place of happiness within yourself (whether you are single or in a relationship), and everything else will fall into place.

The importance of discipline

It might appear counterintuitive at first to say that discipline is key for a happy and fulfilling life. After all, isn't happiness about fun and carefree living? But without some perseverance to push through the tough times, as well as conscious appreciation of the beauty around you in your day-to-day environment, the experience of happiness will be short lived. Creating and continuously regenerating happiness, and being responsible for it on a daily basis can be hard work, let's be honest!

A key driver to the level of discipline you will naturally bring to the situation is your determination to want to be happy. Where does happiness feature on your list of priorities, specifically in comparison to the desire to complain about what's not going the way it should? There is something very satisfying about being able to blame the circumstances and the environment for the predicament that we are in, rather than taking full ownership and responsibility for ourselves. It's strangely comforting to feel sorry for ourselves and be a passenger of our life story, rather than taking the driving seat. Having the discipline at that moment to not be the victim, to instead step up and take charge of our happiness, can be tough, and requires quite a bit of determination.

So yes, not letting anything deter you from being happy requires persistence. That is why, unfortunately, there is no avoiding discipline when it comes to creating and sustaining a state of happiness. However, it becomes much less daunting when you have a clear focus. That's why it is so important to choose your focus once you have finished reading this book. Choose the secrets that speak to you the most and will make the biggest difference in your life. Committing to just a couple of things will set you up for success on your journey to happiness, and will make it much easier to be disciplined.

Your choice, your responsibility

The knowledge that happiness is your choice is a big deal, and will change your life profoundly if you embrace it fully. All of a sudden, you can't blame anything or anyone else any longer. You get the power to choose happiness, and the responsibility that comes with it – which moves you from being a passenger to sitting in the driving seat. You completely own your happiness now! It is your choice alone. But you can't just choose it once. You will have to continuously regenerate and choose happiness, moment by moment, as there will always be things that come into your experience that you won't like. In fact, there will be times when you choose to be angry, upset or grumpy instead – and that's ok, as long as you are aware that it is your choice. You can choose something more uplifting again whenever you are ready.

Children know how to have fun and be happy when they play. During those first years of our childhood, we are intrinsically confident, curious, and always seeking the next big adventure. Somewhere along the way to adulthood most of us lose that happy and carefree way of being, because there is a whole new challenge coming into our lives: responsibilities. But we all still have an inner child within ourselves, that part of us that remembers how to play and have fun. Try to rediscover that curious, fun and powerful person inside you again. Because life is just too precious and too short not to make the most of it!

How to choose happiness despite the circumstances

It's much easier to choose happiness when things are going well than when the circumstances are difficult. The 10 Secrets to Happiness that follow in Part 2 of the book are designed to help when life gets difficult. But for now, I'd like to share with you a very simple yet effective exercise to help you choose happiness no matter what situation you're in.

> **Exercise**
>
> Create a list of 'feel-good actions' – literally, a list of things that feel uplifting when you do them. It might include listening to your favourite band or music track, watching a funny video on YouTube, going for a walk in nature, or taking a break in the sunshine. Whatever it is that makes you feel good and helps shake off thoughts that drag you down should go on your list. Continue to add to your list over a week or two, every time you discover something else that makes you feel good.
>
> Then, the next time you are feeling down, take out the list and see which action appeals to you the most in that moment, and whether it is feasible to do in your current environment. Doing star jumps in an open plan office while shouting "I'm an idiot!" might be a bit radical, but is one of my favourites. It will no doubt turn some heads, but if you can work up the courage to give it a go, it's highly effective, and incredibly liberating. Not taking yourself too seriously helps to deflate a stressful situation, and will remind you in a fun way that you shouldn't take work too seriously either. Choose actions that take just a few minutes and help 'recalibrate' you to a more positive mindset.

And another tip: it is scientifically proven that smiling and laughing triggers the production of feel-good hormones, even if it is faked. So in fact, you don't need to be happy to smile and laugh, but the more you do it, the happier you will feel. And since it is quite contagious, your smile and laughter will very possibly make the people around you smile as well, which in turn will make it much easier for you to keep it going. A smile costs nothing but can make a big difference to your own day, as well as to any stranger in the street. So smile and laugh often, and allow it to help you feel great!

Closing note

Here is the shocking truth: I know the Secrets to Happiness, yet I am not always happy. I still experience anger, frustration and discontentment – and so will you, even after reading this book. Because we are human, and these are important human emotions. So what difference does it make, reading this book and knowing that happiness is a choice? It makes a__ll the difference. Because, simply put, it moves you from being a passive spectator to being in charge of your happiness. Whatever emotion you find yourself in, you will know that you can always, always choose again.

Knowing that happiness is entirely in your control is a big first step on your journey to a happier life. And it's very exciting news! You no longer need to wait for something to change in your life – you can choose to be happy right here, right now. So here is what I would suggest: while you start to explore the 10 Secrets to Happiness, allow yourself to focus on yourself. For once, don't worry about making other people happy – there is no bigger gift that you can give to yourself and your loved ones than to find your own place of happiness and fulfilment. Why? Because you can't make anyone happy – it's their choice, after all. All you can do is to show them how to be happy, by being happy yourself. This book will provide you with a powerful toolkit of ideas, techniques and exercises to experience happiness every day. So enjoy the journey, and remember to have fun along the way!

THE POWER OF
THE UNDERLYING BELIEF SYSTEM

If you believe you can, you probably can.
If you believe you won't, you most assuredly won't.
Belief is the ignition switch that gets you off the launching pad.

Denis Waitley (author and motivational speaker) [4]

What is the underlying belief system?

Life is meant to be a joyful experience full of fun and happy moments. If this is not your current reality, it means some subconscious limiting beliefs are stopping you from living life that way. What if I told you that you are the writer, producer and main actor of your movie called 'life'? The majority of your current movie script was written when you were very young, shaped by your experiences and by what you were told by those around you – your parents, siblings and first teachers in particular. Most of the things you learned were very useful, like the do's and don'ts of modern society, and lifesaving skills like knowing what is safe to eat and what isn't. But there were also a few things you picked up along the way that were less useful, like being told and believing that you are not very bright and interesting, or that you are clumsy. So over time, in those first few years of your life, you started to form a picture in your subconscious mind about yourself, your strengths and weaknesses, and what you thought you could and couldn't do.

This internal map is your underlying belief system, which drives your experience of life. It helps you to navigate through life. It does not refer to any world religion, although if you are religious then your religion is likely to play an important role in it as well. The belief system as referred to here essentially describes your very personal view of the world, and what you see as the truth. Unfortunately for most people, this view doesn't change much once embedded. So unless you have done some form of self-development work since your childhood, there is a good chance that you are currently still acting out the movie script you subconsciously created as a five-year-old. That's the bad news. The good news is that you can change it any time and choose again.

What you believe is what you get

The underlying belief system you hold plays a significant role in how things happen in your life. The time lag between thought and manifestation often makes it difficult to see, but your belief system essentially influences everything you experience. It is particularly important to be aware of any limiting beliefs, as these are very often at the source of problems you are faced with and things that are not going to plan. As the powerful creator that you are, it is your belief system which shapes your reality and what you see as the truth. If you change your underlying beliefs, your reality will change too. Once you know and understand this, it gives you a choice: you can either continue to live as you have been if you are satisfied with your current life, or you can look at your beliefs to see which ones serve you and which ones don't.

Do you know what beliefs you have that are supporting you in your pursuit of happiness, and what beliefs are stopping you from living a truly happy life? Many of these beliefs are well hidden and deeply embedded in your subconscious. You will probably see them as the truth, not recognising that they are simply beliefs that can be changed if they don't serve you. I see it all the time as a coach: whether it relates to health, relationships, money, or any other aspect of life – what you believe is what you get. That is why it is very important to be aware of your underlying beliefs. Learn to replace your limiting beliefs with more positive, empowering ones. Now is the time to choose beliefs and a life philosophy that work for you and empower you!

Example

One of my coaching clients, when I first met him, was very shy and introverted. His biggest limiting underlying belief was 'I am not good enough', which made him think that he wasn't very interesting, smart or funny – and because that's what he thought of himself, that's how he was perceived by those around him. He didn't engage much with his colleagues, so in return they didn't engage much with him either. He thought they didn't like him, and he hated his job. He came to me to find his 'zest for life' again and help him find a new job he'd enjoy more. Once we had identified his key limiting underlying belief and started to work on changing it, it only took a few weeks for him to realise that the people at work were actually very nice, and that there were a lot of things about his job that he really enjoyed.

Now just to be clear – it was still the same job and the same people, it was just his perception that had changed! He started to come out of his self-made shell of insecurity and frustration, and the people around him started to respond to his change in behaviour. All of a sudden, he wasn't the boring, quiet co-worker anymore; he had a positive energy that made him interesting and even fun to be with. He ended up staying in his job and was promoted within less than a year. And all of this happened because he identified his key limiting underlying belief and decided to not be restricted by it any longer. This is what rewriting the movie script of your life can look like.

Common underlying beliefs

Our underlying belief system consists of a mix of limiting and empowering beliefs. I have listed below a few of the common limiting beliefs that I hear a lot as a coach, as well as some empowering positive beliefs (which are unfortunately a lot less common). If any of these sound familiar they might have been playing on your internal dialogue too.

Common limiting beliefs

- I can't do this
- I am not good enough
- I am not worthy to be loved
- People don't like me
- I am bad with money
- I am not very confident
- I am not smart enough
- There's something wrong with me/my body (too skinny/too big/too short/too tall/etc)

Some empowering positive beliefs

- I am perfect exactly the way I am
- I am very talented
- I can do anything
- I love myself
- Money comes to me easily

Now let's assume for a moment that the first, limiting set of the above beliefs represents a person called Emma, while the second, empowering set of beliefs represents Valerie. Can you see just how different their experience of life would be, even when faced with exactly the same situation? Their interpretation would be strongly influenced by their belief system, and the situation would therefore occur to them very differently. A poor mark at school would confirm to Emma that she's not intelligent enough, while Valerie would probably put it down to bad luck and do better next time – after all, Valerie knows she's talented and can do anything, so studying for an exam will come much easier to her than to Emma. A compliment would probably be dismissed as not genuine by Emma, while Valerie would happily accept the compliment and add it as another piece of evidence to her knowledge that she is very good at what she does and perfect exactly the way she is.

Identify your key underlying beliefs

The more empowering and positive your beliefs are in a certain area (e.g. money, relationships, career, health) the more successful you are bound to be in that field. If certain areas of your life don't live up to your expectations, it's a sign that one or several key limiting beliefs are holding you back there. For example, if you have a loving family, a job and hobbies you enjoy, but you are in constant financial trouble, then the area to look at in terms of limiting beliefs is money.

It is a very powerful exercise and well worth taking the time to identify the beliefs that drive the key areas of your life, particularly those that don't work for you. So if you experience financial difficulties, ask yourself: what beliefs do you hold about money, about how easily it can flow to you, or how hard you have to work for it? How much or how little of the big pot is available for you? If you think there is just never enough, it could be the limiting belief that leads you to experience being in debt. If you are struggling with relationships, the following question might be worth exploring: do you believe you are worthy enough to experience love and have a wonderful partner in your life? If your subconscious belief system suggests that you are not good enough, it could either lead to a lonely life where you just never seem to find the right partner, or you could end up in a relationship that is not fulfilling. Your beliefs literally shape all areas of your life, whether you are aware of them or not.

> **Exercise**
>
> Since awareness is the first step to any change you might want to initiate as part of reading this book, I'd like to invite you to spend a few minutes now starting to look at your underlying belief system. When writing your list of current limiting and empowering beliefs, I suggest you consider the following areas, with a particular focus on those areas where things are not going as well as you would like them to:
>
> - Yourself (your personality, intellect, talents, and your body)
> - Your health and fitness
> - Relationships (with your partner; with family and relatives; with friends; with strangers)
> - Work and career
> - Finances
> - Time management
> - Any other areas that you are struggling with
>
> So for example, you might write down 'I care too much about what other people think of me' under relationships, or 'I never have any time to do the things I enjoy' under time management. Make the list of beliefs for each area as long as you like – the more time you can spend on this the better, as you will learn a lot about yourself in the process. Alternatively, if you are

> pressed for time, choose the one area in your life where things are not going the way you want them to, and where you are looking for the biggest improvement. It is very likely that this is the area where your limiting beliefs are expressing themselves the strongest, so it's worth looking for what is holding you back in that area in particular. What are the one, two or three limiting beliefs in that area that are most dominant in your thinking? If you have more than one area that isn't working for you, it's very possible that the same limiting beliefs are at the source of the struggles you are experiencing.

I always find it a very insightful exercise to identify limiting and empowering beliefs with my coaching clients, and try to do it myself every now and then too. If you haven't done it before, I encourage you to spend a few minutes exploring your key limiting beliefs before you start reading Part 2 of the book.

The power of affirmations

Imagine if someone keeps telling you "You can't do this, you're not smart enough". If you heard it often enough, wouldn't you start to believe it? This is an example of a negative affirmation, and how it can, over time, be embedded as a limiting underlying belief. It works in the same way with positive affirmations. Positive affirmations are one of the most powerful tools I have come across as a coach. They are used to 'reprogramme' your brain in a more positive way, to replace negative thought patterns with more empowering ones. I use them with most of my coaching clients, including the client mentioned earlier in the chapter. The client noticed a difference in how he felt about himself and his job within just two weeks of using affirmations (as many coaching clients do), and he was able to fully embed the new, positive way of thinking within less than two months. If affirmations are repeated regularly and consistently, they can make a lasting and profound difference in any area of your life.

How to create powerful affirmations

So what do affirmations look like? Affirmations are simple statements, but there are a few important rules to make them as powerful and effective as possible:

- **Always state an affirmation in the present tense.** So rather than 'I will be interesting and good company', say 'I am interesting and good company'.

- **Always make it a positive statement, avoiding any negation.** The subconscious doesn't understand 'not' and 'don't' – just watch a young child when you say 'Don't touch that'; they see it as an invitation to do just that! So rather than saying 'I am not stupid', say 'I am clever'.

- **Repetition, repetition, repetition.** The secret to success in using affirmations is in repeating them as often as possible, consistently for at least two weeks or until you start to notice a difference. I usually recommend that my coaching clients repeat each affirmation ten times out loud at a time, ideally while standing in front of a mirror, at least three times a day. The more the affirmation is repeated throughout the day, the faster you will notice a difference in your thinking. It is very effective to repeat the affirmations first thing in the morning and last thing at night as well, as that is when the subconscious is most receptive.

- **Act it out – be emotional!** The more emotion and conviction you feel when you repeat the affirmation, the faster it will be embedded in your brain.

- **Keep them short and few in number.** Short, punchy affirmations work a lot better than lengthy statements that are hard to remember. And given the importance and power of repetition, it's better to not do too many affirmations at once – I recommend you work with just a couple of affirmations at a time.

- **Be selective in who you share them with.** It is very effective to share your intentions with a few key people in your life, as it will reinforce your commitment, and give you some encouraging support. However, make sure you only share the affirmations with people who you know will respond positively and support you. Some people are rather negative and cynical about affirmations ("What, you think that's going to work and make a difference?"), which plants seeds of doubt in you that will be very hard to get rid of.

Examples of powerful affirmations

Affirmations are usually designed to address specific underlying limiting beliefs. The following two examples illustrate how this is done.

Example 1

The underlying limiting belief 'I am not good enough' could be replaced with one of the following affirmations (always choose the one that speaks to you the most):

- I am very talented
- I can do anything
- I am very special and unique
- I am perfect exactly the way I am

Example 2

The underlying limiting belief 'I am unattractive' could be replaced with any of the following affirmations:

- I am good looking
- I am sexy
- I love myself
- I am irresistible and magnetic

If you are unsure what your underlying beliefs are, create an affirmation for the area in your life where you'd like to see the biggest improvement. The statement should describe in a short and inspiring way what you want to experience. There are countless possibilities for powerful affirmations, but here are some of my favourites that work very well:

General affirmations to brighten up your day

- I love my life! (this can be adjusted as needed, e.g. I love my job/this project/this task)
- Today is a great day
- Anything is possible
- I choose to see the perfection in everything, exactly the way it is

Relationships

- I am madly in love
- I am in a loving and happy relationship
- I accept myself and all those around me, lovingly and completely

These relationship affirmations work whether you are currently single and looking for a relationship, or whether you are in a relationship that you would like to improve. It's all about getting into the right mindset.

Your body, health and wellbeing

- I feel great!
- I love my body
- I love exercise and healthy food
- I am fit and healthy

Money

- I am a money magnet
- Money comes to me easily and freely
- I am experiencing abundance in all areas of my life

Self confidence

- I am interesting and fun to be with
- I am very good at what I do
- I can do anything
- I am successful in everything I do

Exercise

Now it's your turn. Take your list of underlying limiting beliefs you created earlier in this chapter. Which one or two beliefs would make the biggest difference to you, if you could shift them to something more positive? A very common one is 'I am not good enough', which shows up in different ways in many areas of life, for a lot of people. Then write down a positive affirmation of how you'd like to 'reprogramme' your brain, what you'd like the new, empowering belief to be. Use the above guidelines, 'How to create powerful affirmations', to make the affirmation as powerful as possible.

If you are not sure about your limiting beliefs, choose an affirmation from the list above or make your own, for the area you want to work on. Say the affirmation out loud and check in with how you feel when saying it – do you find it inspiring, exciting, and stretching? A bit daunting perhaps, too? Then it's probably the right affirmation for you. You can define up to about five affirmations in total, but it's more effective to just work with a couple at a time.

Read them out loud to yourself, with conviction and emotion, as often throughout the day as possible. When using the mirror, make sure you look yourself in the eyes while saying the affirmations. This might feel a bit weird at first, but it makes the exercise more effective because you engage three sensory organs at the same time: you speak, hear and see what you are saying. Watch how your perception regarding your chosen area starts to shift within just a couple of weeks. It really is true – the more you hear something, the more you will believe it's true, and since you are the creator of your reality, you get to decide what's true for you!

Closing note

A reader of my blog once asked: "Why am I always so sad?" The simple answer is: if you are sad, it's because you are thinking sad thoughts. If you are angry, it's because you are thinking angry thoughts. And your underlying beliefs are a key driver to the thoughts you think. That's why I am very passionate about the power of understanding the underlying belief system, and using affirmations to create a more enjoyable and empowered life experience. When I take on a new coaching client, helping them to identify their limiting underlying beliefs is always one of the first things I do. It provides a lot of insight on why things aren't working and what is holding them back. But you don't need an expensive coach to map out your limiting beliefs and start to change them. Use the guidance in this chapter and give it a try. I promise it will be quite an eye opener to see how certain beliefs rule your life and shape your experiences. And even more so, what a difference affirmations can make in your life within just a couple of weeks!

This is the end of Part 1 of the book. You now have a great foundation to start living a life you love. You know that happiness is your choice, how to manifest your desires, and how your underlying belief system shapes your current experience of life. And with the powerful tool of affirmations, you can reprogramme your limiting beliefs and start changing your current life experience. Now all you need is the 10 Secrets to Happiness, and you will become unstoppable in living the outrageously happy life you were always meant to live!

PART 2:
THE 10 SECRETS TO HAPPINESS

Building on the empowering context created in Part 1, it's now time to introduce the 10 Secrets to Happiness. Be open minded. Spend at least one day per chapter, and experiment with the ideas presented – see for yourself what difference each secret could make in your life. Once you have reached the closing chapter, I will ask you to choose the one, two or three secrets at most that have made the biggest difference to you, and I will show you how to embed them into your daily routine. You came into this life to have a happy, joyful and fulfilling experience, and what follows is a menu of simple but highly effective techniques to show you how. And don't forget: have some fun!

1ˢᵀ SECRET: CHOOSE WHAT IS

*If you change the way you look at things,
the things you look at change.*

Wayne Dyer (author and spiritual teacher, 1940–2015) [5]

What does it mean to 'choose what is'?

If you had the choice between living your life or living someone else's life, which would you choose? Would you choose the glamorous life of the rich and famous, or the life of your next door neighbour because he's always happy and having fun? A rather hypothetical question, I know, but a very important and powerful one to contemplate nonetheless. Are you happy with your life as it is at the moment, exactly the way it is? This first Secret to Happiness is one of my favourites and listed first for a reason: if embraced fully it can completely transform your life. It is beautiful in its simplicity of just three words – choose what is.

What do I mean by that? Make peace with how things are. Make peace with the people and circumstances in your life, exactly the way they are. Stop expecting them to be a certain way, because here's a simple truth: your circumstances and environment will never be perfect. Family, friends, job, partner, children, house, car, health, money – there will <u>always</u> be something that isn't the way you think it should be. So let go of the notion that something is wrong, and make peace with the way things are, exactly how they are, right now. Let go of the 'it should be' a certain way, and move into the peaceful space of 'it is'. Werner Erhard (author and speaker) summarised it well: "Life is a rip-off when you expect to get what you want. Life works when you choose what you got."[6]

This first secret plays a fundamental role in experiencing happiness, day by day. It applies to the small things as well as the big things. Observe yourself, and see how often you are let down by something or someone because of what you expect to happen, because of how you think it 'should be'. Can you start to see how much freedom it would give you, if you could let go of any expectations and instead embrace the beauty of what is there, exactly the way it is?

How we avoid choosing what is

'Choosing what is' is a great concept in theory, but much easier said than done. In reality, we spend much of our time fighting our current circumstances and attaching labels of how things should be. Before you can fully make peace with your environment, it's important to understand some of the most common ways you might currently resist choosing what is.

1. Complaints

You will know for certain that you haven't yet made peace with your current reality if you have a complaint about it. Complaints represent non-acceptance of what is, and are the most obvious way to resist choosing what is. And it gets even worse: complaining, without taking action, actually creates more of what you don't want. Why? It comes back to the Law of Attraction: complaining keeps you focused on the negative and gives what you don't want additional energy and focus, which reinforces its existence. Or in other words, the more you complain, the more you attract things to complain about. Interesting, isn't it! This means you have three options when dealing with a complaint:

1. Take action to change the situation
2. Walk away from the situation (if feasible)
3. Make peace with the situation as it is (choose what is)

Anything else – particularly continuing to complain without taking any action – is a waste of energy and makes the situation worse. So resist the temptation to join others in complaining about what's not working. Do something about it, walk away, or choose it as it is!

2. Trying to change others

Is there a certain habit that really annoys you about someone close to you, something specific that you have tried really hard to change about them, without success? That's another way to avoid making peace with your current reality. Let me save you a lot of grief and frustration, and tell you something that took me many years to learn, both as an individual and as a coach: people don't change unless they want to change. Whatever it is that is bothering you about them – stop trying to change them and get over it already! Stop expecting people to be a certain way, and instead embrace them exactly the way they are. If someone changes, it is because they want to, not because you are pushing them into it. And no, even your dedicated love for them won't change them, unless they want to change.

Neale Donald Walsch (author and speaker) said it well in *Conversations with God – Book 3*: "What you resist, persists. Denial of something is re-creation of it, for the very act of denying something places it there."[7] In other words, the more you fight against what you don't like, the more likely it is to stay the same. So make peace with the way people are, and learn to love and appreciate them with all their flaws and shortcomings. I am pretty sure that once you stop fighting it, you will start to see new, positive aspects about them that you didn't notice before because you were too busy focusing on what you didn't like. And not only that – I see quite often as a coach that people choose to change their ways precisely because the people around them have stopped nagging and pressuring them into something.

3. Holding on to grudges and resentments

A third habit that might stop you from making peace with your environment is holding on to grudges and resentments. It is quite astounding to observe how long some of us can hold on to age-old arguments, sometimes blocking certain family members or former close friends out for years due to a seemingly unforgivable mishap in the past. Forgiveness is a key part of making peace with what is, so forgive if you need to forgive, for your own sake. Allow the past to stay in the past, and move into the here and now. Embrace the other person exactly as they are, in this very moment, without making them wrong about anything. Interestingly, you will notice that the person that will benefit the most from your forgiveness is not the other person, but yourself: you have subconsciously been carrying around your anger and resentment towards that person everywhere you went, ever since the argument started. Here is a well-known Buddhist story by Zen master Tanzan to illustrate this point:

One warm, sunny spring morning, two monks – one young and one old – were traveling to a village far from their monastery to do some trading. In the high mountains where they lived, there were only small trails between villages, no roads and few bridges. After walking a distance on a narrow, steep trail, the two monks came upon a fast moving stream where a young woman stood on the edge of the bank, afraid to cross. The young monk reminded himself that he had vowed never to touch anyone of the opposite sex. He nodded to the young woman as he passed her by, lifted his monk's robe up slightly and carefully began to cross the stream. But to the young monk's amazement, the elder monk picked up the young woman and carried her across the water. When the old monk put her down on the far shore, she bowed respectfully to him in thanks, and the monk gave her a bright smile.

As the monks continued their journey, the young monk considered and considered and reconsidered the elder's action back at the stream. With each passing mile his thoughts grew angrier and angrier until, hours later, he stopped in his tracks, flush with rage. He shouted and sputtered at the old monk, "You broke your sacred vows! You were never to touch a woman! How can you forgive yourself? You should not be allowed back to our monastery!" Surprised at this outburst, the old monk turned to face him. "I put that woman down hours ago," he said. "Have you been carrying her all this time?"

What a great story. The old monk decides to take action to deal with the problem at hand, and makes peace with his breaking of the vows right away. In the meantime, the young monk carries a heavy load of anger and resentment for hours – and he might continue to carry that load around with him for days and weeks to come, unless he is willing to forgive the old monk. And while this decision will probably not make much difference to the elder, it is critical for the young monk as it is the only way for him to regain his internal place of peace. The story illustrates beautifully that forgiveness benefits the forgiver more than the forgiven.

> **Exercise**
>
> Is there anyone you feel angry or resentful about, because of something they did or said in the past? Something the culprit might even have long forgotten about? Give it a try; forgive what you need to forgive, and experience just how good it feels to let go and have those people back in your life again!

There is one very important point worth clarifying here: forgiving does <u>not</u> mean that you are endorsing what is happening, or giving it your seal of approval. There are some awful things happening in the world. When you forgive and choose what is, it does not mean that you agree with these events. You simply make peace for yourself with what has happened or what is happening right now, in the same way that you acknowledge that you have a name, a body, and look a certain way. In other words, you don't attach any meaning to it; you simply accept it as the way it is. This is what 'choosing what is' is all about, taking all judgement and emotion out of a situation and allowing it to just be. It doesn't mean that you have to stand on the sidelines and just be an observer either. Once you have accepted it the way it is you can reclaim your power to start to influence and change things that can be changed, if you choose to do so. The difference is, now you can take action from a place of empowerment, rather than frustration and anger, which means you have the Law of Attraction on your side to make a positive contribution.

How to choose what is

As long as you fight against circumstances and look for what's wrong, it's difficult to find a place of happiness. So let's take a look at a few simple techniques to learn how to make peace with what is.

1. **Whatever other people around you do, it's not about you.** This is an important point that will help you to accept people and their actions as they are. The people around you are simply absorbed with their own lives, and probably don't even realise the impact their words or actions have on you. Just like you, they are trying to survive, and trying to win the game called 'looking good and avoiding looking bad'. And if they do hurtful things, it's because they have been hurt by others in the past. Nobody is born devious, mean or evil. Learn to see them as the frightened little children they used to be and still are, deep down, and it will become much easier to embrace even the most annoying people in your life.

2. **Nothing is inherently positive or negative – it's all a matter of perspective.** You will find true power when you embrace this viewpoint. We have a tendency to attach labels of 'good' or 'bad' to everything we experience. But the truth is, things just are. We are born, we live, we die – that's life, and what nature intended. Stop judging situations as positive or negative; situations just are what they are, until you attach a meaning and label to them. Start seeing the beauty and perfection in everyone and everything exactly as it is. The weather is a great example: we say it's 'bad weather' when it's raining, but is it really? Think of what a difference the rain makes to nature, how quickly everything goes green again after a dry summer. It's refreshing and nurturing. So next time it's raining, don't call it a miserable day – it's just a bit wet, that's all!

3. **Be aware of your expectations.** You can only get disappointed if you have certain expectations that don't match the reality,

that look at the 'how it should be' rather than the 'how it is'. When you stop judging circumstances as how they should or shouldn't be, you can truly start to embrace them exactly as they are, and the sense of peace and wellbeing that comes with it is absolutely priceless. It will get you well on your way to experiencing happiness!

If you have tried all of the above and still can't make peace with something, look at what it is that you personally get out of not making peace with the situation. Because I promise you, at a subconscious level you're holding on to it for a reason, and getting something out of it in return, otherwise you would have let it go a long time ago. Secret 4 'Get off it' goes into this in more detail.

Example

When our daughter was born, I completely underestimated the challenge of looking after a demanding baby, particularly in the first few months after giving birth. I thought that surely it couldn't be that hard, given all the families with children in the world. But the lack of sleep started to get to me after a while, and even though I was on maternity leave I couldn't seem to find even just thirty minutes to myself during the day. Each day went by in a blur, busy with preparing meals, cleaning and tidying up, taking her out, trying to make her go to sleep for her daytime naps – and then all of a sudden it was 6pm already and time for dinner and the bedtime routine. One evening, after another long day, it occurred to me that even though having a baby was what I had always wanted, I was not at peace with my current situation at all. In fact, as much as it pains me to say it, I was starting to get a bit resentful about not having any time to myself anymore.

Luckily, that's when I remembered the powerful coaching concept of choosing what is, and decided that it was time to stop feeling sorry for myself. I reminded myself that things were perfect exactly the way they were. The truth was, I was having an amazing time with my baby daughter, and she was very good at playing on her own for a while as long as I was in the same room. So I made a conscious decision to make peace with the situation, and embrace every aspect of it. I stopped complaining about it, and instead focused on all the positive aspects of the situation. I chose a simple affirmation to support the change of perspective: 'I have plenty of time to myself'. It was astounding to see what difference it made to choose the situation as it was and no longer complain about it. Not only did I appreciate and enjoy the time with my daughter much more again, I also seemed to suddenly find lots of small pockets of time here and there throughout the day for a bit of me-time!

> **Exercise**
>
> Now it's your turn. Make a list of the key people, situations and things in your life that you think should be a certain way, different from how they are at the moment. Then pick the one that is most on your mind. Make a decision to embrace it exactly as it is – make peace with the way the person, circumstance or thing is right now, exactly as it is. See the perfection the way it is, and accept that it was meant to be that way for a reason. Maybe you even asked for this person or situation before you came into this world, to facilitate a certain learning you were keen to experience. If you can see the learning in every challenge you face, and the perfection of the situation, you are well on your way to owning your happiness no matter what the circumstances. And as you let go of the should be's and allow it to be exactly as it is, tune in and notice how you start to feel uplifted as a result.

You will know if you are doing it right by how you feel, because there is a big difference between 'choosing what is' and just being resigned about it. The former is a powerful choice, and puts you in a place of strength. You will feel good as a result, and it will give you a sense of peace and freedom. When you are resigned to something, you haven't chosen it; you have simply given up hope that it will ever become the way you want it to be. However, you still believe that it should be a certain way – different from how it is at the moment. You will feel stuck and dissatisfied as a result. So make sure you tune in to your feelings and make peace with the situation, rather than just giving up on it.

Make peace with yourself

When it comes to making peace with your current reality, choosing yourself exactly the way you are is possibly the biggest challenge of them all. Many of us run a continuous internal dialogue where we judge everything and everyone around us, but particularly ourselves. Have you ever listened to your internal dialogue, the constant commentator in your head? The voice that might say: "I'm too old for this", "There is no way I can do that" or "I can't believe I just said that!" That's your inner voice. That inner voice can take a trivial little incident, and continue to beat you up about it for hours, sometimes even days, weeks, months or years. As a coach, I have heard many examples of what people think of themselves, and what their internal dialogue entails. Honestly, some of the things we say to ourselves we wouldn't even say to our worst enemies!

Imagine the freedom it would give you if you were able to simply be ok with yourself exactly the way you are, and be ok with every action and every decision you ever took. It is amazing how often we are our own worst critic – it's time to become your biggest advocate and best friend instead! Here are a few tips on how to choose yourself exactly the way you are:

1. **Nobody is perfect, not even you.** One of the main reasons we reject ourselves is because we think we need to be perfect. We have to remember that we are all human, and that it is our imperfections that make us so. Embrace who you are, be clear about who you are not, and show some compassion for yourself. Stop blaming yourself for any shortcomings or flaws you think you might have. What stories are you telling yourself about what's wrong with you?

   When I was four years old and my little brother was born I was thrilled – and devastated. Somehow I made up the story that he was born to make up for my shortcomings (mostly the fact that I was a girl rather than a boy). On a subconscious level, I lived most of my childhood and early adulthood believing that I had failed my parents. To prove my worth, I worked extra hard at school and university, which, admittedly, set me up well for life. However, the underlying driver was the belief that I had to prove to everyone that I wasn't a failure. It took me many self-help books and self-development seminars before I realised (really and truly) that I didn't need to prove anything to anyone. That I was perfect with my imperfections, exactly the way I was. This insight, that I didn't need to prove myself and could just be me, was so powerful and liberating that I quit my well-paid job in the financial services industry. I sold all my furniture and most of my other belongings, travelled around the world for a year, and completely changed my career focus as a result. That's how powerful it can be to let go of the need to be perfect, and instead embrace the unique and amazing individual that you are.

2. **Stop trying to please others.** This is a second important area to tackle to make peace with yourself. Most of us are run by a subconscious fear that we are not good enough, and that the only way to be accepted by society and the people around us is to fit in with their point of view of who we should be and what we should do. We crave being loved and liked. But it is hard work trying to second-guess what others might want and how to please them, and it is simply impossible to please everyone anyway. So instead, just be yourself. You are a unique individual, a powerful, gorgeous, fun-loving and resourceful soul in a human body, and you came onto this planet to experience your expression of self. You are needed the way you are. Be true to yourself, and you will be an inspiration to those around you to have the courage to be themselves too.

3. **We all have our ups and downs.** This sounds very mundane, but it's important to acknowledge that everyone has good and bad days. We all have days where we are feeling great, and other days where we just want to be left alone – this is another important part of what we call being human. Even once you have finished reading this book and know all the Secrets to Happiness, there will still be the occasional day where you just don't feel up for it and just want to stay in bed. The secret is to stop thinking that there is something wrong with that, and instead fully embrace it to be able to move out of it swiftly. Embrace your lack of energy on those days and take it easy. Allow any grumpiness to come out (a little advance warning to the people around you might be advisable), and watch how quickly it will dissipate if you stop resisting it. Because what you resist persists!

Example

One of my coaching clients had a big issue with the shape of her face. She was a beautiful, intelligent and interesting young girl just finishing university, but she wasn't able to see any of her attractive attributes. She had been so obsessed with the shape of her face for the last few years that she had become very insecure, and had accumulated a lot of 'evidence' consisting of comments and looks from people that confirmed to her that her round face was unacceptable. In fact, it was so bad that she was considering plastic surgery. Luckily she didn't have the money for it, so that was ruled out. Unable to take action to change her face or walk away from the situation, the only option left to her was to make peace with the situation as it was.

We worked together on identifying her underlying limiting beliefs, and identified some powerful affirmations to help her change her perception about herself. Yes, the shape of her face was rather unusually round, but – if she could learn to fully embrace it – it would make her stand out from the crowd, in a beautiful way! Embracing her seeming imperfection as part of who she was took a little while, but she eventually learned to choose herself exactly the way she was. I have lost touch with her since, but I wouldn't be surprised if she has become a fashion model, because that's how much of a difference it made in her confidence and appearance when she finally fully embraced all parts of herself.

Exercise

Make a list of every aspect about yourself that you're not happy with – whether it's regarding your looks, your skills, or your personality. Then pick the one that you currently have the biggest issue with, and make a decision to embrace it exactly as

> it is: make peace with the way you are, exactly as you are. Whether it's a big nose, a clumsy demeanour, or a sense of humour that's too dry for most – see the perfection of it, and accept that it is meant to be like this for a reason. Remember, you chose yourself and your life! Once you have tackled the biggest issue, the remainder of your list will become much easier to address. Go through it and make peace with all the other things you aren't happy with about yourself. Embrace yourself and all your attributes exactly as you are. And as you let go of the should be's, tune in and notice how you start to feel lighter with each aspect of yourself that you allow to be exactly as it is. Start to see the awesomeness of who you really are!

Closing note

When I first wrote about choosing what is on my blog (www.secrets-to-happiness.com), I received a lot of feedback. It seemed I had hit a nerve with my audience. Many readers loved it, but some were concerned that 'choosing what is' meant that we would stop challenging ourselves and others, and therefore stop growing. One reader put it this way: "Choosing what is and making peace with it sounds great. But what about continuous improvement?" (He's an Operations Director; can you tell?) A very valid question! It comes back to the three choices you have when dealing with a situation you don't like: take action, walk away (if feasible), or choose the situation as it is. If taking action is an option, take action! But sometimes there is simply nothing you can do about a situation, and you can't just walk away from it either. That's when making peace with what is will save you a lot of unnecessary frustration.

I also noticed that some of my readers thought they had made peace with a situation, but they had actually just given up on it. Deep down, they still thought that things should be different from how they were at that moment. How did I know? Because they were upset and felt disempowered, which is not at all what 'choosing what is' feels like. You will know when you have truly chosen what is, because you will feel uplifted as a result. There will be a deep sense of peace and freedom. So tune in to your emotions – it's only if you feel good that you have fully chosen the situation as it is and made peace with it.

2ND SECRET: BE IN THE MOMENT

Realize that the present moment is all you ever have.
The past only exists in your memory,
and the future only exists in your imagination.
Make the <u>now</u> the primary focus of your life.

Eckhart Tolle (spiritual teacher and author)[8]

What does it mean to 'be in the moment'?

Do you ever wonder at the end of a day, week or month how it went by so quickly? When I was a child, school terms seemed to last forever, and holidays, birthdays and Christmas took decades to come around. Now, as an adult, it feels like days blur into weeks and months, and as soon as Easter is over, Christmas is almost at the doorstep already. How is it possible that time goes by so much quicker as an adult than it used to do as a child? I think it's because children are much better at living in the present moment. As we get older, we start to accumulate baggage of past, present and future thoughts and worries, which makes it increasingly difficult to live in the here and now. By the time we're adults, we're not really 'here' anymore most of the time. We're spending most of our time in our head, thinking, worrying, analysing, planning – basically, we're mostly completely missing the present moment!

Being in the moment is a concept also known as 'mindfulness'. It means being fully focused on the now, letting go of any distracting and negative thoughts that might take you back into the past or let you worry about the future. It means to be fully aware of and experience each moment, and taking in its beauty and uniqueness. When you are fully in the now, there can't be any worry or anxiety, because worrying is focused on future eventualities. There can't be any stress, because stress is triggered by a comparison of where you are and where you think you should be. There also can't be any guilt or regret, because those emotions focus on the past. When you are fully in the present moment, all comparison and analysing stops. There is nowhere you need to be other than where you are right now. Like little children are so apt at demonstrating, there is just the beauty of the moment, and nothing else. The song of a little red robin, a ray of sunshine peeking through the window, or the calming sound of rain on the roof – even the most simple sounds and observations become special and delightful, because you are fully experiencing their uniqueness and magnificence, moment by moment.

Example

When I walk to the train station in the morning on my way to work, I am often so absorbed in my thoughts that I run on complete autopilot. I might be thinking about the day ahead at work, a specific challenge I am dealing with, or what to cook for dinner. I am not paying any attention to anything around me, and often don't even notice what the weather is like unless rain is falling on my head. It is very different when I am present in the moment. When I am focused on the here and now, I notice things. Lots of things! I use all my five senses to experience the moment. I consciously breathe the fresh morning air, and take in the different smells of my surroundings. I can hear the birds singing in the trees, and see a happy dog chasing after a ball in the wet grass. I watch the sky and notice beautiful cloud formations, and see the birds flying in the wind on a breezy morning. My fifteen minute walk to the train station suddenly feels like a little holiday, refreshing to mind, body and soul. When I arrive at the train station, I feel grounded and happy. At this point, not even a cramped rush hour train full of grumpy commuters can dampen my mood. I am ready for a great day ahead!

How to practise being in the present moment

The challenge of being in the present moment is to find a way to stop the analysing brain, the never-ending chatter and commentary in your head. When we analyse something, our mind either takes us back into the past – for example to compare this beautiful moment to another moment we've experienced before – or sets off our imagination about the future, what's coming next. In other words, thinking takes us out of the present moment. But how do you stop thinking and worrying about the past, present and future? There are a few useful techniques that can help you deal with some of the main distractions that might keep you from being in the present moment.

1. Let go of the past

One of the biggest distractions keeping us from fully experiencing the 'now' is the time we spend contemplating the past, whether it's what happened five minutes or ten years ago. Have you ever listened in to your thoughts and internal dialogue, to see how much time you are focusing on the past? Most of us spend an incredible amount of time analysing, reviewing, assessing and reassessing instances from the past, looking at them from various angles and often giving them a negative meaning which is usually not an accurate reflection of reality. It might be very little things like analysing why that person on the train looked at you funny, or how embarrassing it was not being able to remember your neighbour's name when you passed him on the street. Or it might be a presentation that you think you didn't deliver as well as you could have done, or something inappropriate you said in front of your colleagues that made everyone laugh, which you experienced as hugely embarrassing. Everyone has their own unique stories going round in their head, but the underlying pattern is the same – they consume a large amount of thinking time.

It's only when you let go of the past that you can be completely present in the here and now. So start to pay more attention to the kind of thoughts that are going through your head. Notice when you are reviewing a situation from the past, and make peace with any negative occurrences that are still running through your head now. Realise that whatever negative meaning you have attached to what happened is just your interpretation, your story. There are any number of different ways that this particular incident could be interpreted, so choose a positive one instead. Make peace with what happened, using the principles of Secret 1. Leave the past in the past, and start to see the beauty of the present moment.

2. Learn to embrace death as part of life

Now this sounds incredibly depressing: to embrace death. But the truth is, most of us live life as if we will live forever. We postpone living our dreams until tomorrow – and then the day after that, and the day after that – thinking that we will find the time to make them a reality at some point in the future. As paradoxical as it might sound, it is the acknowledgement that death is certain which teaches us how to be truly alive. You might die tomorrow, who knows? So stop ignoring death, and embrace it as part of life. Imagine the urgency it would create if you lived each day as if it was your last. Would you choose to have the same insignificant argument with your partner or children at breakfast, if you knew it was your last conversation? Or would you just let it go and instead tell them how much they mean to you, how much you love them? Embracing death and realising that you don't live forever is a very powerful concept. Remind yourself often of the gift called life you've been given. Enjoy each day as if it was your last, because one day it will be!

3. Rediscover your inner child

Children know how to be in the here and now. I first came across the idea of the 'inner child' while exploring the Hawaiian healing technique Ho'oponopono with Ihaleakala Hew Len, but more and more psychologists and therapists today acknowledge the importance of the inner child. Our inner child is part of our subconscious, and represents the child we once were. It's the playful part within ourselves that represents our innocence and purity. It also holds all our key memories of when we were hurt, disappointed, angry or sad. It is a very powerful exercise to visualise interacting with your inner child. There is so much power in remembering that you used to be a toddler once, and that you still have that inner child within you. We seem to grow up thinking that in order to be a proper adult we have to be serious and hard working, and that there is no more room for idle play time. I say remember your inner child, reconnect with that important part within yourself, and rediscover how much fun it is to be in the here and now!

Example

When I first heard about the 'inner child' I had reached a crossroads in my life, where a high-flying career without a deeper purpose was no longer a priority. I was feeling somewhat restless and disconnected, searching for something more without even knowing what I was looking for. The first time I tried to connect with my inner child, it took quite a while before I was able to find her. After all, I hadn't known she existed, and had been busy with my career for years without giving her any attention. I sat quietly, with my eyes closed, and simply tried to visualise what she would look and be like (basically a four-year-old version of me). At the beginning, she was incredibly shy and would hardly even come to me to say hello – that's how much I'd been neglecting her. I spent several weeks visualising her every day and spending time with her, to allow us to get to know each other.

It felt so good when she finally gave me a proper hug, and it still brings tears to my eyes today thinking about it. Even though it all just happened in my imagination with my eyes closed, it felt like I had just found a part of me again that I had lost without even knowing it. Psychologically, this symbolic act of the inner child (the subconscious self) fully embracing, accepting and reconnecting with the adult (the conscious self) is a very important step in the process of becoming a grounded and happy grown-up again. It truly nurtured my heart and soul. I felt full of energy, ready to take on the world, or just do some mischief. I felt fantastic! Today, when I visualise her as I go for a walk, I see her dancing and running around the trees, in such a joyful and carefree fashion that it always brings a smile to my face.

In my line of business, where I guide organisations through large transformation projects, I am known as a very rational, analytical and no-nonsense person. So I am perfectly aware that the above sounds a bit far-fetched – it is all happening in my head, after all. I don't know what you will see or feel when you try to connect with your inner child, and whether your experience will be anything like mine, but I know that the connecting with my inner child feels very real. She also keeps surprising me, showing up in unexpected places and doing fun and creative things I would never have thought of, which suggests to me that she's not simply a figment of my imagination. Since reconnecting with my inner child I feel a lightness and playfulness about my life again that I wouldn't have found without her. So give it a try, and see what mischief your inner child might inspire you to.

> **Exercise**
>
> Close your eyes and see if you can visualise your inner child – think of it as a four-year-old version of you. Give yourself time to tune in to yourself and find your inner child. I promise you it's there, but it might take a little while before you can feel and see it. Observe and find out whether the child is in a happy place or feeling sad and lonely. Spend some time together, show your inner child how much you care and love it, think about some fun activities, or ask the child what it would like to do today – you might be surprised by what it comes up with! Try to spend a few minutes each day, while you are commuting to work for example, to meet and connect with your inner child. Tune in to that playful side of yourself, the toddler inside you who can't wait to come out and have some fun. The stronger your connection with your inner child becomes, the happier you will feel.
>
> And how will you know that visualising and connecting with your inner child is real, and not just you making it up? Trust your intuition. If it feels uplifting and makes you feel good, then it has touched the right places inside of you.

If you find it difficult to visualise your inner child, spend some time observing how young children interact with their environment, how they can totally be in the moment and be completely absorbed by whatever it is they are interacting with. There is no space for thoughts about the past or the future; there is just the here and now. And they are having so much fun! Start to see the beautiful, the miraculous, in everyday occurrences as they do. Take thirty minutes to walk one block like toddlers do, marvelling at everything – the symmetry of a flower, the busy life of a bee, the wonders of a puddle, the beauty and uniqueness of each pebble on the pavement. Enjoy the beauty and uniqueness of today, because there will never again be a day quite like this.

Other ways to be in the moment

There are many other ways to get into the present moment. Ultimately, it is all about finding a way to switch off the brain for a moment – to be rather than to think. Meditation works very well for this purpose. Since we can only think one thought at a time, focusing on something very simple like your breathing is very effective. Just observe how you breathe in and breathe out, how it feels, and how relaxing it can be to do nothing else but that. When other thoughts creep in (and they will), just acknowledge them and let them go again. This basic form of meditation is called 'conscious breathing' and can be done anywhere and anytime. Some of my other favourite activities to bring me into the present moment include going for a walk in nature, spending time with our daughter, or watching the squirrels in our back garden when they are out to play.

Exercise

How do you get 'into the moment'? What do you have to do or not do to just be? Spend some time every day over the coming week experimenting and practising being in the here and now. It might be on your way to work, during your working day, or once back at home – no matter where you are, I promise you that

> being in the moment will make a profound difference to how you feel and how you experience your day. Focus on what you are doing, and what is happening around you. Don't think, just be – and experience life, in this very moment. Savour it like a delicious dessert, moment by moment. Because this is your life, here and now.

Closing note

While finalising this chapter I've been focusing on consciously spending time in the 'here and now' every day. I have to admit I was amazed to discover how little time I actually spend in the present moment these days. Whatever the activity, whether at breakfast, on my way to work, while food shopping or doing the laundry – I always seem to be completely absorbed in my thoughts and running on autopilot. So it made a big difference to spend even just a few minutes each day focusing 100% on the present moment. I switched off the constant chatter in my head and just enjoyed and experienced life right here, right now. What a difference it made! The number of new things I discovered as a result on my daily commute is astounding. And the best thing is, focusing on the present moment also lifts my mood every time, right away.

There is something magical about fully experiencing the present moment and noticing the beauty of the little things that normally get overlooked while rushing through the day. Dare to be playful, have some fun, and watch how contagious it can be for those around you. Life is a magical adventure, and it is such a waste not to make the most of it every moment of every day. It's time to take a break from all the thinking and treat yourself to a mental mini-holiday!

3RD SECRET:
STOP WORRYING, FEELING GUILT AND REGRET

*There is nothing for you to go back and live over,
or fix, or feel regret about now.
Every part of your life has unfolded just right.
And so – now – knowing all that you know
from where you now stand,
now what do you want?
Go forth in joy, and get on with it.*

Abraham (channelled by Esther Hicks)[9]

What are worry, guilt and regret all about?

Worry, guilt and regret are probably some of the most counterproductive emotions we experience. Worrying is thinking about eventualities and possible negative outcomes in the future. Feeling guilt and regret focuses on perceived negative events from the past. The big question is: why do we spend so much time beating ourselves up about things that happened long ago, or thinking about the potential eventualities of what might, maybe (though probably not), happen in the future? Surely it must be obvious that all of this is a waste of time and energy, and that there are much better ways to spend our days. Unfortunately these emotions seem to be an intrinsic part of human nature. Over the last few years I have been exploring why we experience worry, guilt and regret, and have found some very interesting answers.

1. Evolution

Nature doesn't make mistakes, so experiencing guilt, regret and worry must play a specific evolutionary role. One of the big advantages of experiencing guilt and regret is that they offer learning opportunities for growth. Each situation presents us with a chance to analyse what we have done, decide for ourselves the best course of action if the same happens again in the future, and walk away from the situation a wiser person. The ultimate learning then would be to realise that this is all there is, and that once we have learned the lesson we were meant to learn from the situation, we can (and should) make peace with the past and leave guilt and regret behind. Similarly, worry can help us prepare for future eventualities and make sure we are as ready as possible for what's coming. But again, the learning here is to realise that worry does not serve a purpose beyond planning and mentally preparing ourselves, and we simply need to accept that things will unfold exactly as they are meant to unfold – and, of course, how you have vibrationally lined them up for yourself through your thoughts.

2. Forgiveness

An alternative or perhaps additional explanation is that guilt and regret serve the purpose of helping us to learn about forgiveness, and in particular learning to forgive ourselves. Kabbalah and 'A Course in Miracles' are just two of several schools of thought that feature forgiveness as a centrepiece of their teachings. According to these philosophies, one of the reasons why the world exists is to explore and learn about forgiveness. Knowing that we are here to learn and grow from our mistakes makes it easier to let go of guilt, regret and worry. This means that once we have learned our lesson, we can choose to let go of the negative emotions and move on.

3. Freedom of choice

The third explanation I have found while investigating these questions comes from the Law of Attraction. As the powerful creators that we are, we have been given complete freedom of thought as our platform for joyful creating. The world truly is our oyster! Whatever we want to do or achieve in life, if we really put our mind to it, we are unstoppable. In fact, we have so much freedom that we can choose thoughts that bind and restrict us, like guilt, regret and worry, until we decide to choose differently and go for something more empowering. For some people on this planet, this takes up most of their lifetime unfortunately, and they only realise at the end of their lives (or even after they've transitioned back into the non-physical) that it was their choice to make. Don't make the same mistake; use your freedom of choice to stop worrying, feeling guilt and regret, and focus instead on experiencing more happiness in your life!

How to deal with worry

Winston Churchill said it well: "When I look back on all these worries, I remember the story of the old man who said on his deathbed that he had had a lot of trouble in his life, most of which had never happened." Worrying is all about playing different scenarios through in your mind about how the future might unfold. Worry keeps you from experiencing the present moment fully and from living a happy and fulfilled life. So what is the best way to deal with worry and get rid of it? Here a few suggestions to consider:

- **Realise that the more you worry, the more energy you give to that specific thought, and therefore the more you are bringing that negative future into your reality.** When you worry, you are essentially planning and mapping out an undesired future, and – as per the Law of Attraction – the more attention you give it, the more likely it is to become a reality. I find this point alone powerful and scary enough (I really would rather not manifest the things I worry about!) to help me let go of worry, and replace it with more positive and empowering thoughts.

- **Remind yourself that everything is perfect exactly the way it is.** If everything is perfect, and will unfold exactly the way it is meant to, there is no need to worry, ever. In Neale Donald Walsch's *Conversations with God – Book 3*, he talks about how more advanced societies in the Universe understand that there is a process which ensures that everything unfolds exactly the way it is meant to. They understand that all things are perfect, and that worry therefore does not serve any purpose. All they need to do is not interfere with the process.[10] I like the idea, and it intuitively makes sense: the more spiritually advanced a society, the less worry there is.

- **The loudest arguments happen in your own head, and your greatest opponent is yourself.** The vast majority of things you worry about are fabrications of your own imagination, and just serve the purpose of stopping you from playing full out and being your biggest and best self. Over the years as a coach, I have seen too many examples of people living a small and unfulfilled life because of their internal arguments with themselves, and the low opinion they have of themselves. Stop letting that voice in your head keep you from going after your dreams. Dare to take some risks! Because at the end of your life, it will be the most scary things you did that you look back on most fondly, and the things that you didn't do that you will regret the most.

- **You can only hold one thought at a time.** If you are a worrier by nature and none of the above help to reduce your tendency to worry, remember that you can only hold one thought at a time. So next time you worry about something, consciously decide to focus on your breathing or a positive thought instead to occupy your mind.

Do you spend a lot of your worry time thinking about other people? You might worry about the people you love, because you want to see them safe and happy. And you probably also worry about complete strangers, though in a different way – what might they think of you, if you do this, or wear that? So here are two additional tips to specifically help you stop worrying about other people:

- **Life your life, and allow others to live theirs.** If you have children, you probably spend a lot of your time worrying about them, in one form or another, no matter what their age. I know you do it out of love, but – keeping the Law of Attraction in mind – all it does is send negative energy their way. Instead remind yourself that, just like yourself, they came onto this planet to express themselves, have a joyful experience and learn some lessons along the way so they can grow into the person they are meant to be. Don't get in the way of their expression of self, their experiences and their mistakes. The best thing you can do is to fully stand behind them and be excited for them, and support them in learning and growing into the amazing individuals they are meant to be. And of course, the same applies to any other people in your life you care (and worry) about!

- **Stop worrying about what other people think.** We all worry about what other people might think of us, to a greater or lesser degree. And we often adjust our behaviours accordingly, trying to 'fit in'. But here's the thing: this is a complete waste of time. Why? Because everyone around you is in exactly the same predicament as you, worrying about what everyone else around them might think. So just drop the worry about what other people think – they're likely to think something completely different anyway, which most probably has nothing to do with you at all. Instead, do more of what you want to do!

Exercise

Pick one thing currently on your mind that you are worried about and think about a lot. It might be something related to work, your family and friends, your health, your financial situation, or anything else that has been occupying your mind. Get clarity about the worry by writing it down on a piece of paper. Very often, the monster is a lot scarier in the closet than once it is out in the open – by verbalising the worry it might just turn out to be a complete non-issue when you look at it in broad daylight. If it is still a worry, go through each one of the above points to help you let go of it. Can you feel a heavy load lift off your shoulders?

How to deal with guilt and regret

While worry is focused on future eventualities, guilt and regret focus on what has happened in the past. Of all the species on this planet, we are most likely the only one that keeps banging on (and on and on) about things that have happened in the past. Whatever it is – it's time to close the chapter and move on. Here is a simple four-step approach to let go of guilt and regret:

THE 10 SECRETS TO HAPPINESS 81

1. **What can you learn from the situation that you feel guilt or regret about?** Take on the learning and commit to embrace it fully going forward, so that the same situation doesn't happen again. Nobody is perfect, and we all make mistakes. Or better said: we are all perfect exactly the way we are, and all mistakes are in fact our opportunities and playground to learn and grow.

2. **Is there any action you should be taking?** Is there someone you should apologise to, or is there anything else you can do to make amends? If the answer is yes, commit to taking the action, right away. The longer you procrastinate, the longer the guilt or regret will linger and remain stuck with you.

3. **Forgive yourself and anyone else you need to forgive in order to be able to let it go and move on.** As long as you haven't made peace with the past, you will recreate it in your present and future again and again. If the situation from the past involves other people, clean up with them what you need to clean up. Apologising for past actions often opens up the space for the other person to see the mistakes they have made, too. But have no expectations of how they will respond – whether they apologise as well or prefer to remain stuck in their story of 'being right', let this be about you and what you need to do to let go of the past. Say what you need to say to forgive yourself and others, and free yourself from the burden at last.

4. **Then drop it and move on into a new future.** Once you let go of the guilt and regret you can finally move on. You can stop thinking about the 'should have done's' and instead appreciate what you have, right now. From now on, whatever you do, be fully in the here and now, not stuck in past memories. No more guilt or regret!

If you are in the unfortunate position that the person you feel guilt or regret about has passed away without giving you the chance to clear things up, write a letter to them instead. I promise you, they will hear you, and had already forgiven you the moment they passed into the non-physical.

Closing note

So let's summarise the facts: worry, guilt and regret are in your conscious control and are some of the most counterproductive emotions you have. They don't add value beyond the learnings they hold, and keeping the Law of Attraction in mind, they keep you focused on what you don't want and therefore bring more of that into your experience. They can also stick around for a long, long time, and – if left unaddressed – can lead to serious illness and depression. It takes some mental discipline to let the negative emotions go, forgive yourself and others, and focus on more positive thoughts instead, but it is possible and entirely in your control. Understanding the true costs associated with experiencing worry, guilt and regret is an important driver to helping you let these emotions go.

I like the following quote by Neale Donald Walsch, from his book *Conversations with God – Book 2*: "All events, all experiences, have as their purpose the creating of opportunity. Events and experiences are opportunities. Nothing more, nothing less. It would be a mistake to judge them as 'punishments from God', 'rewards from Heaven', or anything in between. They are simply events and experiences – things that happen. It is what we think of them, do about them, be in response to them, that gives them meaning. Events and experiences are opportunities drawn to you – created by you individually or collectively, through consciousness."[11]

Reminding myself of this fact helps me to let go of guilt, regret and worry much more quickly.

Every now and then, we get completely consumed by what's not working in our lives. But now you know that whatever you focus on will grow in your life, so it is time to start paying more attention to what _is_ working in your life. Worry, guilt and regret have been lingering long enough – let them go! I hope that the tips in this chapter will help you to experience the growth and learning as well as the incredible joy and freedom that comes from releasing these negative emotions. Learn the lessons that these opportunities are offering to you, and then move on and start to focus on living the life you truly want and love. And next time you are faced with a difficult or challenging situation, look for the positive in it. See the learning in all adversity, and you will shift and transcend any difficult situation very quickly.

4TH SECRET: GET OFF IT

*The trouble with troublesome people is
that they often have much to teach to those they trouble.
Love 'em all,
The Universe*

*P.S. Fortunately, they're no trouble at all, some even go away,
once your lessons are learned.*

One of the daily 'Universe' messages sent by Mike Dooley
(www.tut.com)[12]

What does it mean to 'be on it'?

Do you ever find yourself in a bad mood, for no apparent reason? I've always wondered about the causes for this phenomenon. What is the thought process in our head that decides to flick a switch and puts us in a bad mood? What causes us to wake up grumpy in the morning, when there's no obvious reason to be ill humoured? I believe that in the vast majority of cases it's because we're 'on it' with something. What do I mean by that? It means we have a complaint about a person, situation or circumstance which makes us angry, upset or frustrated, or any other shade of negative emotion. And the complaint is so big and persistent, that it sometimes becomes the first thing we (subconsciously) think about when we wake up in the morning, making us feel grumpy without even knowing why.

Maybe you're 'on it' with your job because you think it's incredibly boring, or with your partner because he or she is so annoyingly stubborn and just doesn't understand you. Whatever your recurring complaint might be, there are perfectly valid reasons (and undeniable facts, no doubt) that justify your frustrations. Nevertheless, they still show that you are 'on it'. Why? Because no situation is inherently negative, so you could find 'counterevidence' which is equally factual, if you were willing to look for it. It's your choice. And if you have any persistent complaints in your life, it means that until now you have chosen the more painful route of being 'on it'. But the good news is, you can always choose again, and 'get off it'. This chapter will show you how.

Example

I have suffered from lower back pain for many years, and had been complaining about it for just as long. And I have a ten-minute exercise regime, which – if done daily – pretty much keeps the pain away. Problem sorted, you say? Unfortunately not. You'd think that it would be easy to find ten minutes a day to do some back exercises, particularly if they make such a difference to my comfort levels. But I used to resist doing them, just as much as I used to resist the back pain itself. As a coach, I knew very well that all I needed to do was to find a set time in the day and make the exercises part of my daily routine. But I didn't seem to be able to decide on a time that worked for me. I was resisting it so badly! So I ended up thinking of the exercises, and not doing them yet again, day after day. I was incredibly skilled at finding the perfect excuse every single day.

It was only while I was writing this chapter and thinking of a good example that it struck me: I'd been 'on it' big time – poor old me and my terrible back! I was so attached to my persistent complaint about my back pain, that I had subconsciously chosen to stick with the 'poor me' drama rather than strengthen my back and fix the problem. Sounds ridiculous when you look at it like that – why would I choose to be in pain, just to be able to stick to my story and feel sorry for myself? But it's actually quite a common phenomenon. It's only when you truly look at and understand the cost involved with a persistent complaint that it becomes obvious and urgent enough to let it go. And that's what I did, right then and there. I finally committed to stop complaining and do something about it. After all, I just had to find a ten-minute time slot, which – with all the noise and resistance about it removed – was really no big deal. I made it part of my evening routine, and soon it became an established habit I didn't even think much about anymore. And I felt so much better for it, with the exercises strengthening my back and keeping the pain well at bay.

How to get off it

Let's say you're really annoyed with your partner, because he keeps complaining about things, and it seems it's always your fault. He's just had another go at you about something insignificant, and you are fuming, and are about to plunge headfirst into a big argument. But then, at the last moment, you catch yourself and realise that you're on it with him, big time. What do you do now? The first and most important thing, which you've just done, is to realise that you're on it, that you're angry, upset, frustrated, or whatever the emotion might be. Asking you at this point to follow Secret 1, 'Choose what is', will usually not be very well-received; you're just too emotional about it. And in a very weird way it is a satisfying place to be, to know that you are a poor victim – even if it's at the cost of your own happiness. When you are truly angry or upset, the best thing to do at this point is to distract yourself, to focus on something else entirely. Maybe you could go for a walk and get some fresh air? You will find that when you look at the same situation again a few hours later, it is often much less dramatic and much easier to do something about.

Once your emotions have calmed down, it's time to look at things from a more rational perspective. What follows is a menu of suggestions on how to deal with complaints like the one above that you've had for a long time. You might find that one suggestion works particularly well for you, or you might prefer different suggestions for different situations. Give them all a try if you can!

1. Choose being happy over being right
2. Don't take things personally
3. Understand your underlying motivation
4. Be aware of your assumptions
5. See it as an opportunity to grow

Let's look at each one in turn.

1. Choose being happy over being right

Are you 'on it' with a person in your life about something they have said or done to you in the past? It might be something that just happened a few hours ago, or it might have happened years ago. We have an incredible talent for storing incidents like these in our long-term memory, and holding them against the people in our lives, especially our loved ones. A few years ago, I used to work as a volunteer at the Landmark Forum weekends in London. Sitting at the back of the room and listening to the participants' stories, it struck me how often it happened that someone stopped all communication with a close friend or family member because of a disagreement. And many of these disputes went on for years! Sometimes we are so determined to prove that we are right and the other person is wrong, that we are willing to sacrifice our happiness for it.

I distinctly remember one man who had stopped all contact with his mother for over ten years because of a big argument. During the seminar, he realised just how much this disagreement had cost him in terms of his happiness. He was convinced that his mum – who was just as stubborn as he was – would not let the argument go, but he decided to take action anyway and call her. I don't know what he said to her, but she got onto the next plane to be with her son and get him back into her life. That's all it took after over a decade of disagreement and radio silence – the willingness to let it go, and a phone call! It was beautiful to see mother and son together again on the final evening of the seminar. And this was not an isolated instance; the Landmark Forum facilitated the reuniting of many friends and family members every time, and continues to do so around the world.[13]

I am not sure why we hold on to grudges like that for so long, but it is definitely a very human thing to do, and it happens all the time – even if not quite to the extent of the example above. The key is to realise the impact it has on you and the relationship with the person you hold a grudge against. If you have fallen out with someone, take a look at the situation. What is it that caused the two of you to fall out? What would happen if you said "I'm sorry, will you forgive me?" You might say it wasn't your fault, and there is nothing for you to apologise for – if anything, it should be the other person apologising. If that is the situation, then you are currently choosing to be right over being happy. All the facts show that you are in the right, and that there's no reason for you to make the first step and do what you might consider humiliating. And I'm sure you're right! But what would it take for you to let go of the anger you're holding anyway? What would happen if you apologised and said whatever needs to be said to let it all go and get the other person back into your life? That's what choosing to be happy over being right looks like.

> **Exercise**
>
> If you have fallen out with someone, or in other words, are 'on it' with someone, take a look at the situation. What is it that caused the two of you to fall out? Make a conscious decision to get off it, and say "I'm sorry", or whatever you need to say to break down the barriers. It's time to get that person back into your life, the way it used to be!

2. Don't take things personally

I've said it before, and I'll say it again, because it could make such a difference in your life if you truly believed and acted on it: whatever the other person says or does to you, it's never about you. It's always about the other person, their own story and drama, so don't take what is being said personally. It's just not worth your time and energy. Just acknowledge that whatever they just said or did is something they needed to deal with as part of their drama, and let it go. For example, let's say the woman behind you at the supermarket checkout gives you an angry look because she thinks you're not packing your items into your bags fast enough. While your meticulous style of packing might have been the last straw to trigger her reaction, I can assure you that the underlying reason for her angry response was caused by some completely unrelated issue she had been thinking about long before she stood in the queue behind you.

Of course, it's easier said than done to not take things personally. It's particularly hard to not get upset when someone is throwing some nasty words at you. But here is an interesting fact: did you know that you are much more likely to get upset about statements that you think are true and agree with, consciously or subconsciously? So for example, if someone calls you 'fat', but you are perfectly happy with your body, the insult is unlikely to bother you. You might even find it amusing! However, if you've been struggling with your weight, or have been working hard to make that little belly disappear, you are much more likely to take it personally. The same would apply if someone called you stupid, ugly or lazy: you will only feel offended if you think (correctly or incorrectly – it's all about your own perception) that there is some truth to it. Give it a try if you don't believe me. If an insult strikes a chord and upsets you, then it's not about the other person; it's about you coming to terms with whatever shortcomings you think you might have. A little confidence booster would be a good idea, for example by using affirmations (see 'The power of the underlying belief system' in Part 1). Remember, you are unique and perfect exactly the way you are.

And finally, if all else fails, consider whether this is a battle worth fighting for – does it really matter what the other person just said to you, or how they treated you? Trust me, it's just not worth your precious time and happiness, so this is yet another reason not to take it personally, and get off it instead.

3. Understand your underlying motivation

If you can't make peace with a person or situation, look at what it is that you personally get out of 'being on it'. It's not something that you do consciously, but unless there is some sort of benefit to you, you would have stopped being upset about it long ago. So for example, it might allow you to be right, or it might make you look like a victim which gets you sympathy and extra attention from other people every time you share your story. Maybe the story is just too good to stop telling it! But now look at the costs associated with continuing to be at war with that particular circumstance. It probably costs you energy, happiness and love for yourself and others, at the least. Then compare what you are getting out of it with the costs: is it worth it, continuing to hold on to the anger or frustration? Once you are fully aware of the costs, you will most likely find it much easier to get off it and let the anger and resentment go.

In this context it is also worth mentioning that every now and then, you might simply not want to get off it, and just need to spend some time being miserable – and that's ok! As long as you're aware that this is your choice, and that you can always choose again, you can stay in your 'poor me' drama for as long as you want and need to be. You might say, why would anyone want to do that? But I've seen it again and again, how important it can be for someone to just be in that space of grumpiness, anger or frustration for a while, with any attempts of outside help failing miserably. It is one way of emotionally processing a situation and getting to terms with it. Usually, people will come out of it eventually, when they're ready. If they don't, it might be time to make this book their next birthday or Christmas present!

4. Be aware of your assumptions

The reasons to be 'on it' are usually mostly fact based – or so we think. But are they really all facts? What assumptions are you making, filling blanks where you don't have enough information? It is important to be fully aware of any assumptions you are making, because, by their nature, assumptions could well be wrong. For example, let's say you get off a train and the man standing in front of you on the platform looks at you, then starts laughing at that precise moment. Wouldn't you automatically think that he is laughing because of you, and that there is clearly something wrong with you? Maybe it's because of what you're wearing (you knew it didn't look quite right when you checked yourself over in the mirror this morning; you should have chosen a different outfit!). Or is there a hole in your jumper somewhere that you didn't notice? Or who knows, maybe you've got some toothpaste on your cheek? You need to get to a mirror, and quick! But of course, all of these thoughts are based on the assumption that he's laughing because of you. Only if you had asked him you would have found out that you just reminded him of a character in a movie he watched last night, which made him remember a funny scene that made him laugh out loud.

It is astounding to see how much grief we cause ourselves because we interpret the actions of others in a certain way (i.e. make assumptions). Incorrect assumptions are very common and are bound to cause completely unnecessary misunderstandings and frustration for all parties involved. So catch yourself when you are making an assumption, and ask questions to clarify the situation whenever you can. Remember that everyone is unique, which means that people don't just look different, they also act and think differently. Assuming that they are following the same thought processes as you therefore only leads to confusion and grief – particularly between men and women, who are wired very differently. Make sure you are really clear in your communication, both in sharing what you are thinking and wanting, and in understanding where others are coming from. This will make a huge difference in how often you get on it, and how much easier it becomes to get off it.

5. See it as an opportunity to grow

If all else fails, and you find it hard to get off it, try to see it as an opportunity to grow. Remind yourself that there is no such thing as a negative experience, that it is in your power how you interpret what happened. When you see annoying people or situations as opportunities that are presented to you as a learning, it usually becomes a lot easier to let go, simply because there is now a bigger, 'wiser' context to the situation. Kabbalah and many other schools of thought teach that it's the difficulty in any situation that is the truly positive aspect of it, because that is where the light is hidden. In other words, it is within your biggest challenges in life that you will find your biggest learnings, and it is those learnings that bring you the peace and happiness that you are looking for. So from now on, when you're about to get on it, choose to see the problem as an opportunity instead, and fully embrace life's difficulties. And then just watch and see what difference this change of perspective can make to your experience.

When I first took this on many years ago, and made a conscious decision to see every problem as an opportunity, I was blown away by the difference this change of perspective made. A delayed plane departure became an opportunity to have an interesting conversation with a stranger; a shortage of cash when I first moved to London led to creative new ways of exploring the city – it's amazing what beautiful places you can find by walking around without aim and allowing yourself to get lost! I didn't know about the Law of Attraction back then, but it was of course a very powerful way to shift the focus from an issue to more positive aspects of the situation. And in the same way that more complaining brings more things to complain about, it's equally true that the more positive your thinking, the more you attract things to be positive about.

> **Exercise**
>
> To start to reprogramme your brain and observe the power of words, practise replacing the word 'problem' with 'opportunity' every time you come across it today. Observe what it does to how you look at the situation, how it affects your creative process in finding a solution, and how it changes your feelings towards the situation, too. The shift in perspective should make you feel more empowered, and the situation is bound to appeal to you more when you see it as an opportunity rather than a problem – there is a pull effect towards an opportunity, whereas the natural reaction to a problem is to run away from it. So play with these two words for a while, and see what difference it makes!

Closing note

Here I am, telling you all there is to know about how to get off it. Does that mean I'm never on it? Absolutely not (just ask my partner). But knowing about the techniques shared in this chapter helps me to let go of my frustrations and complaints much more quickly and effectively. While I might have held on to an argument or complaint for days on end in the past (I am very stubborn by nature), I now catch myself quickly, and a few hours later it's all long forgotten. It has improved my quality of life significantly, and made my days much more joyful and light-hearted.

So next time you're angry or grumpy, you will finally know what's going on. Will that make you any less angry, or less grumpy in that moment? Probably not. But it gives you a choice. When you are ready to do so, establish what you are 'on it' about. Use the suggestions from this chapter, and see what difference they can make to help you let it go. Once you get off it, your mood will be lifted immediately, which will allow you to get on with your day in a much more enjoyable and empowered way.

5TH SECRET:
GIVE YOUR LIFE A PURPOSE

Here's the truth. We exist on this earth for some undetermined period of time. During that time we do things. Some of these things are important. Some of them are unimportant. And those important things give our lives meaning and happiness. The unimportant ones basically just kill time.

Mark Manson (blogger and author)[14]

Why do we need a purpose?

Let's start by clarifying a common misconception: you don't need to prove anything to anyone, and there is nothing you have to be or do to justify your existence. You are worthy exactly the way you are. All that matters is that you are yourself and that you enjoy life.

But here's the thing: for most of us that's not enough. Without a purpose or a goal, something is missing. What if you came onto this planet and into your specific life and circumstances for a reason? It is up to you to decide what you want to do with your life and your talents. There is nobody else like you on this planet – nobody else sees the world the way you see it and experiences it in the same way you do. Considering this fact, it seems a waste to just live day-to-day with a job that pays the bills, without contributing to something bigger, something that's important to you.

What you choose to do doesn't have to save the world. It doesn't even need to be anything that other people think much about. Because this is about you, and nobody else. Having something that is important to you and that you care about will give you direction. And when you are inspired to take action, when you get the satisfaction of knowing that you are doing something that is important to you, it will bring you a sense of achievement and fulfilment like nothing else can. In turn, this will make you happy, because a fulfilled and happy life go hand in hand. Studies have shown that people who have found a purpose and created meaning in their lives are happier and more satisfied with their lives. It feels good to have a purpose, to have direction and work towards something that you care about.

Pushing through the fear of failure

Many people get scared when it comes to thinking big and really going after what they are passionate about. The fear of failure stops many from even trying, leading them to live a small life to keep it safe. I know what I'm talking about, as I was one of them too. I was always quite ambitious and a hard worker, both at school and at university. It worked out well for me, and I managed to land a prestigious job as a management consultant with McKinsey, one of the top three strategy consulting firms worldwide. My career took off nicely, and by the age of twenty-eight I was a senior manager at a financial services company in the City of London. If someone had told me then that I was playing it too safe because of a fear of failure, and more specifically, my fear of disappointing the people I care about the most, I don't think I would have taken them seriously. I was a young, successful woman with a great career – what could possibly be wrong with that? It was only a few years later that I realised how I had never really failed at anything. Great news, you say? No, it was actually quite sad news. It meant I had always played it sufficiently safe to never fail at anything and embarrass myself, or disappoint anyone. It only occurred to me then that failing is not a sign of weakness, but a sign that you are on to something big, if you just keep going. Becoming my own boss and writing this book were two of the big ventures that happened as a result. If you truly believe in yourself, anything is possible.

Thomas Edison famously made 1,000 unsuccessful attempts at inventing the light bulb before he had the big breakthrough. When a reporter asked, "How did it feel to fail 1,000 times?" Edison replied, "I didn't fail 1,000 times. The light bulb was an invention with 1,000 steps." Another great example of what is possible when you keep pushing through any adversity and failure is the actor Sylvester Stallone. He had a rough childhood, and didn't fare much better as an adult. Without a job and with no steady income, he had to sell his dog for $25 to help pay his household bills. Two weeks later he wrote the *Rocky* script, in a record three days. He tried to sell the script, but was rejected repeatedly, again and again – allegedly over 1,500 times. Imagine what it must be like to be rejected that many times, and still keep going! But Stallone believed in his script and in himself. Eventually, after some improvements to the script and continued perseverance, he was offered $125,000, but only if Stallone would *not* star in the movie. Although his bank balance was barely $100, Stallone refused. The offer was increased to $250,000 and then an unprecedented $350,000, but he still would not accept unless he starred in it. Now that takes some guts and vision! Finally, United Artists agreed. They allowed him to play the role of Rocky, but would only pay him a $35,000 salary and a percentage of profits as a concession. He accepted. Incidentally, Stallone's first purchase with his $35,000 was buying his dog back for a whopping $15,000. The movie *Rocky* cost $1.1m to produce, and grossed an astounding $200m. Its six sequels grossed over $1bn in total, and today *Rocky* ranks fourth on the American Film Institute's list of the '100 most inspiring films of all time'. Sylvester Stallone has become a legend in the film industry, and even his dog became famous as Rocky's dog Butkus.[15]

Anything is possible when you decide to play full out and keep going no matter what. But you can only win the big game (whatever that game is for you) if you allow yourself to step out of your comfort zone into the unknown and take some risks. Learn to see your failures as an opportunity, a lesson learned and a stepping stone that brings you another step closer to achieving your goals. Nothing can stop you if you really, truly go for it. Any boundaries or limitations you currently experience are of your own making, and you can push through them whenever you are ready to step out of your comfort zone. Any limiting beliefs you might have, let them go now and just go for it. Life is too precious and too short not to!

Exercise

Go back to the limiting beliefs you identified while reading the chapter 'The power of the underlying belief system' in Part 1 of the book. Take a look at your list, and see what has been holding you back from living your life full out so far. Which of your beliefs have been keeping you small, playing it safe, rather than living a life full of excitement, passion and fun? Two very common indicators of a hidden fear of failure are worrying about what other people might think of you and the fear of disappointing those you care about the most. In fact, chances are that all beliefs that make you play it safe are simply the fear of failure in disguise.

To start with, pick one thing, large or small, which would push you out of your comfort zone, but would be great fun to do. It might be something you've always wanted to do but felt too

> scared to do, or something you've just come up with while reading this chapter. This exercise is about exploring what it is like to step beyond the limiting beliefs that keep you in check, and having some fun. A friend of mine took on this exercise and went on a dinner date in a restaurant in London just wearing sexy underwear and a coat. She sat at the table all evening wearing the coat, and it was just her and her date who knew that she was wearing nothing but underwear underneath. She had the best time ever, feeling sexy and adventurous, and it certainly ensured a very interesting conversation with her dinner date. What fun, adventurous or silly challenge would you like to take on for yourself to push your boundaries?

Selfless or selfish contribution?

Is it wrong not to aspire to be another Gandhi or Mother Teresa? One of the biggest worries I had when I started to look for my purpose in life was thinking that I would have to give up my little luxuries to make a contribution to the world. After all, isn't it selfish to put my own wishes first? But here's the thing: unless you focus on your own happiness and fulfilment first, you don't have anything to give to anyone else. It all starts with you. You can't contribute to the world without looking after yourself first. So focus 'selfishly' on feeling good and going after your passions, because only when you feel good first can you make others feel good too and make a true contribution. You might have been taught that fulfilling other people's needs is more important than fulfilling your own needs, and that it is selfish to look after yourself first. This is particularly true for women born before the 1980s (Generation X, Baby Boomer Generation, and older generations). But unless you do what you are passionate about – rather than what you think you should be doing because it is expected of you – you won't be able to be yourself and live the fulfilling life that you came into this world to experience. Don't let the world miss out on you. Let me say it again: you are truly one of a kind, so allow yourself to be you!

While a 'selfless contribution' means that you put everything and everyone else before you, a 'selfish contribution' means that you put yourself first while still making a difference in the world. How does that work? If you do something for yourself that you are very passionate about, you will feel great as a result. By doing what you love doing, your energy and drive become contagious, and you become an inspiration to others. You make a difference to the community by sharing yourself and sharing your positive vibe – what better contribution can there be than to share your happiness? So think about what makes your heart sing. Once you have found something that is important to you and start taking action towards it, the people around you will benefit from it naturally, because of the feel-good magnet you become. And as someone who is truly committed to living your dreams, your example will inspire those around you, and make a bigger difference in their lives than any self-sacrifice ever could.

Example

I struggled for a long time to get clarity on my purpose in life, both because of my fear of failure as well as because I didn't feel very inspired by the idea of having to make a selfless contribution and putting myself last. Many seminars and books I had been exposed to over the years suggested that I choose a purpose bigger than myself, something that would make a real difference in the world. Some recommended choosing one of the big problems in the world, like world hunger, war victims, terrorism, domestic violence, homelessness – there are quite a few to choose from – and making a contribution towards solving one of these. All of them are very worthy causes and certainly a great commitment to take on. However, as selfish as it might sound, I wasn't really interested in that. I was looking for something that was important to _me_, that I enjoyed and that would improve my quality of life. I wanted to make a difference in the world, definitely, but it had to first make a difference in my life. That sounds rather selfish, doesn't it?

I looked back over the different jobs I'd been doing over the years, and saw a common thread emerging: I am passionate about working with people, and in particular to help them identify and make the most of their potential. This was true as a strategy consultant in the early years of my career as well as in my years as a senior manager, and it's what inspired me to become a professional coach and business change consultant. I continued to explore and experiment with different ideas, until it finally hit me: I wanted to live an outrageously happy life, and help other people do the same! I still get goosebumps today when I remember that moment of realisation – and it was so obvious when I finally discovered it, as if it had always been right under my nose. At last, I had found a way to make a difference <u>and</u> be selfishly, truly happy at the same time – by exploring, living and teaching the Secrets to Happiness.

What is your purpose?

Now it's your turn – time to discover your purpose! What would you like to do with your unique set of talents, passions, experience and background? What purpose would you like to give your life that gets you jumping out of bed every morning, excited and ready for another day? What follows is a list of five questions to help you kick-start the thinking process. Try not to overthink it though. It's always best to go with your gut instinct on this, because your passion and purpose come from the heart, not the mind. And it is absolutely fine to come up with a purpose that feels 'kind of right', and then refine it over time. The important thing is to get your boat out of the harbour and start sailing; it is much easier to adjust the direction once you are out in the open water and moving. To help illustrate what a possible answer might look like for each question, I have provided my own responses as an example.

Question 1: What are you passionate about?
Before you define your purpose it is very helpful to first understand your passions. What makes you forget time? What makes your heart sing, and puts you into a good mood when you do it? What is it that gets you jumping out of bed in the morning? All of these questions are great ones to explore to find out what you are passionate about. Then distil the essence of it into one statement. Mine reads as follows: 'I am passionate about seeing people empowered and happy.'

Question 2: What one word best summarises you?
Now that's an interesting question. If you had to sum up your talents, your interests, your passions, and what you are about in just one word, what would it be? The first word that comes to mind is often the right one, but it's worth spending a bit of time on this. The word I chose for myself which really speaks to me and sums me up well is 'care': I care about what I do and how I do it; I care about people's happiness; and I care about making a difference in the world. What is your one word? There are thousands of options to choose from, so have some fun with this!

Question 3: At the end of your life, what would you like your gravestone to say about you and your life?
It might feel a bit odd to think of your gravestone, but this is another very powerful question. What do you want the rest of your life to be about? There is not much space on a headstone, so we're

looking for a short statement here. I would like mine to say something along the following lines: "She cared, inspired and made the world a happier place."

Question 4: What would your obituary say about you, after a long, happy and fulfilling life?
Looking back at your life when you are ninety-five years old, what would you like to be remembered for? What would the obituary say about you as a person, and what would it say about your biggest achievements in life, and your legacy? Allow yourself to get inspired by your own life story. Here is an extract of what I'd like mine to say: "Alex Wipf truly lived by her mantra 'anything is possible'. She lived her dreams and made all items on her bucket list a reality – there was nothing she didn't try at least once! She was a gifted author, coach and speaker, and many of her books were on the *New York Times* bestseller list. Her positive outlook on life was contagious, and with her books and seminars she inspired and empowered millions of people to live a happier life." Now just to clarify: at the point of writing this, I am an international nobody. I haven't published any books yet, haven't been invited to give any speeches, and don't hold any happiness-related seminars as yet. But that's my vision of where I want to get to, one step at a time. What does your vision of your life and legacy look like?

Question 5: What would you like your purpose to be?
Now that you have more clarity on your passions, what you stand for, and what you want your life to be about, it should be much easier to define your purpose. What one sentence best summarises what you want your life to be about? Make it something that gives you goosebumps when you read it – both because of the exciting thought of playing your chosen game, and because it's pushing you out of your comfort zone. It's time to play full out! And again, don't worry if it only feels 'kind of right' initially, as you can easily change

and refine your statement over time. I have seen too many people procrastinate for years and years, ending up doing nothing because they wanted to get perfect clarity on their purpose first – don't be one of them! My statement (which is continuously evolving) currently reads as follows: "My purpose is to bring more happiness to the world by inspiring and empowering millions of people to live a happy and fulfilled life." The words 'millions of people' in particular really push my boundaries and take me very much out of my comfort zone (I am quite a private person). At the same time it feels incredibly inspiring, though, and it is the game I am committed to play. What statement will give you goosebumps every time you read it?

Once you are clear on your purpose, decide what actions you'd like to take to start making it a reality. It's the taking of action that will make it real, and show you whether you need to adjust the direction of your chosen purpose or not. If the actions don't make your heart sing, they might not be quite the right ones yet. Just keep exploring, keep taking action and adjust your ship's direction as you go. By choosing a purpose for yourself that inspires you and pushes you out of your comfort zone, you and your talents will truly start to shine. If you are currently struggling to get up in the morning, I promise it will start to become a lot easier once you have found your purpose. People with a purpose need less sleep, because they are fuelled by their passion and their enthusiasm for life. So listen to your heart – it's your mind that is trying to keep you small. Write your purpose down, and put it somewhere where you will see it every day, like on your fridge door. It will help to guide your thoughts and your actions on a conscious as well as subconscious level, helping you to seek out all opportunities as they present themselves to achieve your purpose.

Closing note

It took me quite a long time before I found my purpose, with much experimenting and many adventures along the way. Volunteering was an important part of the exciting process to get clear for myself why I am on this planet, and what contribution I would like to make. I spent three months in Nicaragua, tutoring children in English, Maths and Geography. I had an amazing time, and it was heartwarming and very humbling to live with a Nicaraguan family, interact with the children, and get a glimpse of their daily challenges. Volunteering is a very rewarding way to make a contribution to the world and explore what you'd like your purpose to be. Whether you cook and serve food at a homeless shelter, read a book to a lonely old man in a retirement home, or help build a school in rural Africa – whatever you choose to do, it will make you feel great because you are making a difference in other people's lives. So if you are not quite clear yet on your purpose, then I can highly recommend volunteering. Allow yourself to experiment with different types of volunteer work, and find something you enjoy doing. Who knows, it might even become your chosen purpose!

Having a purpose that makes your heart sing is probably one of the most important ingredients for a truly happy and fulfilled life. And the more challenging and stretching your chosen purpose, the more it will inspire you and help keep you going when the journey becomes a bit tough. As Leonardo da Vinci put it, "Fix your course on a star and you'll navigate any storm." In other words, dream big and you'll be able to push through any adversity. Once you have found your purpose, the real adventure begins. Going after your dreams will make you stand out of the crowd, and push you out of your comfort zone. It takes courage to leave the gravitational pull of the masses behind and be true to yourself. But what might seem really hard at the beginning will get easier quickly. It's like a space shuttle launching into orbit: the shuttle uses more fuel during the first three minutes after take-off than it will need for the remainder of its journey around the earth. So when you are faced with challenges and failure, stick with it and stay true to yourself. It is definitely worth it, I promise. Have fun while pursuing your purpose, because life really is an amazing experience. And always remember: the Universe is on your side and wants you to win!

6ᵀᴴ SECRET: BE INTENTIONAL

If you will let your dominant intention be to revise and improve the content of the story you tell every day of your life, it is our absolute promise to you that your life will become that ever-improving story. For by the powerful Law of Attraction – the essence of that which is like unto itself is drawn – it must be!

Abraham (channelled by Esther Hicks)[16]

What does it mean to 'be intentional'?

What is your first thought when you wake up in the morning? Is it a feeling of excitement about the day ahead, or a sense of dread about yet another dull day at the office? Your thoughts play a key part in how you experience life. Being intentional is a simple yet very effective way to help you guide your thoughts in a positive manner and set yourself up for an enjoyable and smooth running day. It is also a key technique to making the Law of Attraction work for you, and becoming the powerful proactive creator that you are meant to be.

So how does 'being intentional' work? It's very easy: before you start an activity, get clarity on what exactly you would like to experience. Then describe it with a short statement, with as much conviction as possible. So for example, if you're about to make a difficult phone call to discuss a problem, you might say 'I intend to have a productive conversation and resolve the issue at hand'. If you're at reception waiting to be called into a job interview, you could say 'I intend to have a very successful and enjoyable job interview'. Or if you go somewhere where it's notoriously difficult to park your car, it could be 'I intend to find a parking space easily'.

These intentions work on many levels: firstly, setting intentions forces you to get absolutely clear about what it is you want to experience, and increases your level of focus. Hopefully, they will also help to uplift you and see things in a more positive light, which in turn makes the activity easier and more enjoyable. From a Law of Attraction perspective, the intention mentally (and therefore vibrationally) prepares your experience in the way you would like it to unfold. When you then begin to carry out the activity, it already has the 'flavour' of how you want it to be. And the more disciplined you are about setting intentions up front, the stronger the impact. As you develop a habit to use positive intentions throughout your days, things will get easier and easier, and you will feel that you are 'in the flow'. That's why it is such an important tool in the context of the Law of Attraction: setting clear intentions on a consistent basis will speed up the process of manifestation significantly, because the signal you send out to the Universe is continuously aligned with the outcome you are looking for. That's what lucky people subconsciously do automatically – they expect to be lucky, and because of their consistent expectation (or positive intention setting), things flow and happen to their advantage.

Example

When I wake up, even before I get out of bed, I thank the Universe for the great day ahead, and set the intention that I will have a fabulous, enjoyable and productive day. As I head off to work, I set the intention that I will have a quick, safe and enjoyable journey. And while I am travelling, I repeat a few more times: 'I intend to have a fabulous, enjoyable and very productive day today.' I feel positive and excited while I say it – it's a personal pep talk, so to speak, to align myself with the Universe. I continue to set intentions throughout the day, before each meeting, workshop or presentation, as well as ahead of an important phone call. With the bigger things like workshops and presentations, I combine the intention setting with visualising what that 'excellent presentation' will look like, and how it will feel to interact with all the people in the room. This not only focuses my mind on the purpose and objective of the upcoming session, but it also prepares the experience vibrationally in a very positive way.

How to set powerful intentions

Setting positive intentions is no rocket science, and doesn't need to take longer than a few seconds. First, think about what a good outcome of the upcoming activity would look like. What one, two or three adjectives best describe the experience that you want to have? Would you like it to be enjoyable, exciting and fun, or rather quick and productive? I actually tend to use very similar words over and over again for different intentions throughout the day, as you might have noticed in the example above. I find this works really well, as it sets a general theme to my experience of the day, but you can of course be as creative and varied in your choice of words as you like. The important thing is that they represent what you want to experience, and that they make you feel good.

Intentions are very similar in style to affirmations, which means they are most effective when they are short and to the point. So, for example, 'I intend to go on a shopping trip and find the perfect jacket as well as a pair of trousers that make me look great, and are within my tight budget' won't be as powerful as saying 'I intend to go shopping and find something I love and need, at a bargain price'. It's all about getting to the essence of what you want to experience, and this summarises the first statement well. Of course, you need to be clear in your mind what the words mean to you, but too much detail usually detracts, more than adds to, feel-good thoughts. The important thing is that it feels good to say the intention, and that it resonates positively with you.

A final point to keep in mind when setting intentions is that they should always be phrased in the positive. For example, if you say 'I intend to not become upset when I have this difficult conversation', what your subconscious is drawn to is 'upset' and 'difficult'. Why? Because, as already mentioned in Part 1 of the book, we live in an attraction-based Universe – whatever you focus on is what you will experience. Instead, you could say 'I intend to stay calm and have a positive conversation', which describes the desired experience perfectly. So be aware of your choice of words; if you feel uplifted when saying it, you got it right.

Exercise

Practise being intentional today. As you move through the day, be aware when you go from one activity to another, and consciously decide beforehand what and how you want to experience each new activity. Then, using the format 'I intend to ...', say your chosen intention either quietly to yourself in your head, or, if you can, out loud. With a little practice, this whole exercise won't take more than a few seconds at a time. It is incredibly powerful to get clarity on what it is you want to experience, and to mentally predetermine the outcome before it starts.

Beware of subconsciously setting negative intentions

It's not that we don't normally set intentions. We do, quite regularly. However, it normally happens on a subconscious level, and is often negative. For example, if you are about to go into a meeting that you have been dreading for days, you have subconsciously influenced the unfolding of the meeting in a negative way – for days. You might have been worried that things won't go to plan, and then of course the printer has a paper jam and you can't provide paper copies of the report you were supposed to present, which puts you into proper panic mode – you knew something like this was going to happen! So, subconsciously, you were expecting something to go wrong, and so it did. If you had set the intention on the day as 'have a productive and successful meeting', you would probably still have had a paper jam in the printer, but instead of going into panic mode you would have simply improvised and sent the document electronically before or after the meeting. And if you had been setting positive intentions for the meeting from the get-go, rather than dreading it for days, you would probably not even experience a paper jam. You'd be in the flow, and things would most likely run very smoothly – and if there were any hiccups, you'd improvise very elegantly and effectively.

Being in a bad mood is another subconscious way of setting negative intentions. Next time you're in a bad mood, try to listen to your internal dialogue. It's likely to be dominated by negative comments both regarding what is happening at the moment, as well as what is about to happen. And then of course things do go wrong, because that's what you are expecting. So for your own sanity, and to make your days as enjoyable as possible, I would highly recommend giving positive intention setting a try, and being aware of any negative subconscious intentions.

> **Exercise**
>
> If everything seems to be going wrong for you at the moment, there is a good chance that you are subconsciously setting some powerful negative intentions. Try to listen in to your internal dialogue for a day or two, and see what your predominant thinking pattern is. It's very likely that there is a strong correlation between your thoughts and what is happening around you. Those thoughts keep you stuck because they create more of the same; and if you put enough emotion into it, it will get even worse. Spend a few days practising positive intention setting, and see what a difference it will make to how you feel.

Closing note

When I came back from my around the world trip in 2008, I temporarily moved in with a young couple to keep costs down. Their flat had amazing views over Canary Wharf in London, but it soon transpired that the couple were in a difficult personal situation. He was an investment banker who had just lost his job, and had been unsuccessful in finding a new position as yet. Used to a very comfortable lifestyle, it was hard for both of them to adjust to the new financial situation. Arguments became a common occurrence, and I got drawn into their downward spiral of fights and negativity. By the time I moved out and found my own place to live, I was in a very negative space and as far away from 'being in the flow' as I had ever been.

Knowing about the Law of Attraction, I could see how my negativity was causing my experience of 'the worse it gets, the worse it gets': the more I was thinking about negative things, the more negative things I was attracting into my life. Everything was incredibly hard work – I couldn't even get a mobile phone contract, and that says a lot in today's world where you can almost get a free phone with a McDonald's meal! It was a big eye opener to see this side of the Law of Attraction – it really felt as if the Universe was conspiring against me. Everything was going wrong, with one challenge after another being thrown at me. It was exhausting!

As soon as I moved into my new flat, I decided to do some 'mental detoxing'. I started to listen to uplifting Abraham materials again, and peppered my days with positive intentions. It only took a few days before I started to feel more positive again. I wasn't out of the woods yet though – the couple had decided to move out of the flat as well to find cheaper accommodation, and it was (of course!) a very painful process to close that chapter. The landlord refused to release the deposit due to some minor issues with the flat, issues that had happened long before I entered the flat-share agreement. However, I was determined to stay in a positive frame of mind, and rather than arguing my case with the couple and the landlord, I decided to forego my share of the deposit and get out of the situation as quickly as possible.

Why am I sharing all of this with you? Because I want to illustrate a very important point: it takes time for the Universe to catch up with your change in vibration, and it can be very frustrating during that transition period to continue to be faced with negative experiences. Perseverance and a positive mindset are critical to shift the situation to a more positive reality. It took about a month before my negative experiences started to ease off, and I was finally getting back into a more positive flow of things again. So if you are in a difficult situation at the moment, and it feels like the Universe is conspiring against you, don't give up. Use this simple technique of intention setting every day, and remember that there is a time lag in your manifestations. The positive intentions will make you feel better very quickly, and if you persevere and stay positive, then the Universe will catch up with you in no time at all.

7TH SECRET: DO IT NOW

Somebody should tell us, right at the start of our lives, that we are dying. Then we might live life to the limit, every minute of every day. Do it! I say. Whatever you want to do, do it now! There are only so many tomorrows.

Michael Landon (actor, 1936–1991)

What does it mean to 'do it now'?

On an average day, a person has over 50,000 thoughts running through their mind. Of these, the vast majority are the same as the day before. Considering the power of thought, it makes a lot of sense to keep your 'manifestation power hub' as tidy and positive as possible. 'Doing it now' is what I would refer to as 'mental decluttering' – clearing your precious mental space from any dominant recurring negative thoughts which go through your head every day without you taking any action. In essence, it's getting rid of all the should's, ought to's and other procrastinating phrases, and getting on with it!

These recurring thoughts usually sit in one of two categories: the first category relates to things you don't want to do but should be doing. A large majority of these are simple to do's that wouldn't take long to action and could be dealt with easily, but instead keep cluttering up your mind and make you feel guilty because you still haven't done anything about them. Examples include clearing out the receipts in your wallet, mowing the lawn, taking the gas meter reading, or backing up your laptop. If you're like me, it might take anywhere from a few days to weeks or even months to get simple chores like these out of the way. And that's how long they linger and influence your thinking and your happiness, and therefore your power of manifestation.

The second category of negative recurring thoughts relates to things you would like to do but don't because you think you don't have the time or money, or because they push you too much out of your comfort zone. The actions themselves are positive and in fact often very exciting, but because you're not doing them, you're feeling dissatisfied or guilty. This includes all the 'living your dream' kind of activities like driving a supercar, doing a bungee jump, observing the northern lights, or building your own dream house. It also includes more mundane but equally rewarding things like organising a holiday or a long overdue get-together with friends.

'Doing it now' means stopping those niggling thoughts and taking decisive action to start getting the ball rolling. Taking on one, two or three actions a day to either tick off an item completely or get them moving doesn't take long, and is incredibly satisfying. It's just like with physical decluttering: once you tick off those forever lingering and dust collecting to do's, you will start to feel lighter right away, and will probably be inspired to keep on going so you can tick off a few more.

Things you don't enjoy doing, but keep thinking about

Let's say you have a few niggling thoughts about things you should be doing, but you decide that now is not the right time to do them, because you're busy with something else or you just don't fancy doing them. And now imagine you keep thinking about these same little things over and over again, day after day, about how you should get them done. I read in a book once that when you think about something more than three times, take action and do something about it. I really liked that idea. Not that I am actually following the suggestion after only thinking about it three times after all, we have over 50,000 thoughts a day. But after thinking about it repeatedly over a few days it is definitely a good time to take action. And the funny thing is, it very often doesn't take long to do what needs to be done, and you will feel so much better for it!

Example

For about six months, I had a persistent complaint about one of my cosmetic products. It was loose facial powder, and the manufacturer had decided to change the container in which the powder was stored. Admittedly, the product looked more appealing, but the holes that dispensed the powder were now so small that they kept clogging up. Every time I used the powder (which was every morning), the thought kept replaying in my mind, how annoying it was that they made this change, and how I really wanted to send a letter of complaint to the cosmetics company. Not exactly the most motivating and uplifting conversation I was having in my head, every morning – for six months! I could of course have simply bought a similar product from a different brand, but was quite attached to that specific powder. I tried making the holes bigger myself (with partial success), and even went through the trouble of going to a local shop and – hearing that other customers were experiencing the same frustrations – I asked if it was likely that the old packaging would be reintroduced. "Very unlikely," the shop assistant said. So at long last, I finally went to the company's website and logged a complaint. That's all I wanted to do (I thought), complain and see what they had to say about it. Logging the complaint took no more than five minutes. Five minutes, and I had spent six months thinking about it, every single day! A completely insignificant little thing, but it still managed to taint my morning routine. It took another couple of months before it fully sank in that my complaint would definitely not make them reconsider their packaging strategy. I finally changed the product altogether, which is of course what I should have done right from the start, but had been too stubborn to consider.

Now as trivial as this example might sound, I don't think it is an uncommon occurrence. What are the things you keep thinking about without taking action? Maybe you bought a product that stopped working after a day, and you still haven't returned it for a refund three weeks later? Or you keep getting reminders from your dentist that your next check-up is overdue, but you still haven't managed to make the call to book it in? Or maybe there is a small hole in your favourite sweater that keeps getting bigger after each wash because you still haven't fixed it? The potential list is endless. And of course the way to deal with it is simple: Commit to doing it. Then do it. Starting right now!

> **Exercise**
>
> Make a list of your should do's that you have been procrastinating about and that are most dominant in your thinking. Maybe you have a to-do list, possibly one that is so long nothing ever gets done? If so, pick the three items from that list that you think about the most, and take action on at least one of the three items today.

Take inspired action

Once you are ready to take action, it is well worth having the Law of Attraction work in your favour by aiming to be in a positive frame of mind before starting the activity. The more you force yourself and are in a negative place when you take action, the less effective the action will be, as you are essentially trying to swim upstream against the current of a river. Instead, go with what feels good whenever you can, as often as you can, to align the Universe with what you are trying to achieve. To use the analogy of the river again, taking inspired action with a positive frame of mind is equivalent to riding the current of the river downstream – it won't require much hard work from you at all to get it done.

I know this is easier said than done. It is difficult to take inspired action if it's a dull chore or something you don't enjoy doing. Let's say you have a long action list that you need to work through, that you can't ignore any longer. In those situations, I would suggest that you tune in with yourself and find out which of the many actions on your list you feel most inspired to move forward with at this very moment. The simple experience of choice alone very often makes it easier to deal with the task at hand. Choosing the action from your to-do list which inspires you the most will put you into a more positive frame of mind right from the start. It almost feels like you actually wanted to do this (after all, you chose it), and are now giving yourself permission to do it. Approaching something with a positive attitude will make you more focused and more productive, and help to get it done a lot quicker.

Example

I have a long list of to do's. Some of them stay on the list for a very (very) long time, like doing my annual self-assessment tax return. One morning I felt an unusual urge to get stuck into doing my tax return (several weeks before the deadline – almost unheard of!), and even though it was cutting into my writing time, I decided to take this opportunity to take inspired action, and finally get my tax return done. Because I was in a positive frame of mind, what would usually drag on for days actually got done within just a few hours. It felt fantastic to complete this forever lingering to-do item.

Now of course there will be certain things that you simply never feel like doing. If there is a continuous niggle at the back of your mind about something you need to get done, I suggest you schedule an appointment with yourself to tackle it and get it out of the way. Just remind yourself how much better you will feel once it's done.

Stress versus going with the flow

It is worth mentioning the phenomenon of stress here. Did you know that stress is a choice? You can choose to be stressed, or you can choose to be busy instead. The activities are exactly the same; it's just the frame of mind that is different. When you are stressed, your frame of reference is 'there is something wrong here', because things are not going the way you expect them to go. On the other hand, when you are busy, you simply have a lot of things to do, without getting worked up about it or blaming yourself for it.

I mention stress in this chapter for a reason: stress is closely linked to the concept of 'doing it now'. David Allen, author of the book *Getting Things Done*, summarised it well: "Much of the stress that people feel doesn't come from having too much to do. It comes from not finishing what they started."[17] So watch out for any half-finished to do's that are still hanging around, and get them done and out of your way as soon as possible.

You can't get into the flow or take inspired action when you are stressed, because you are essentially fighting with the task at hand. However, if you choose to let the stress go, including any negative stories that came with it, and embrace the task to just get it done instead, you can really get into the zone and go with the flow. This will not only make it more enjoyable, it will also eliminate the negative mental chatter and make you a lot more productive.

Things you enjoy doing, but never find time for

When was the last time you did something you love doing, just for yourself? Like dancing wildly to your favourite music, singing in the shower (no matter what it sounds like), going for a walk in nature, or treating yourself to a massage – there are so many options! We often don't give ourselves permission to enjoy what we love doing the most, because we are so consumed with all our tasks and duties. Take out your 'feel-good' list from the chapter 'Happiness is a choice' in Part 1, and do the things you love and that make you happy. Do them often, ideally every day! I promise you, spending just a few minutes of intensive fun time on one of your favourite activities will re-energise you in a way that will make up for the time manifold.

It is also worth creating a bucket list. A bucket list is simply a list of all the things you want to do and experience in your life, before you 'kick the bucket'. When I first wrote my bucket list, it included numerous travel destinations around the world, as well as many exotic activities like swimming with dolphins, skydiving, wild water rafting, snowshoe walking at night, abseiling, tango dancing, experiencing a medium, and helicopter hiking. And that was just a small part of the list. I have ticked off most of these activities since, and keep adding new ones every year. I have promised myself to do at least one thing from the list each year, ideally more. This year I went hang gliding in the Swiss Alps for the first time. Sailing along mountain peaks like a bird, enjoying amazing views and feeling the thermal winds lifting us up into even greater heights was an extraordinary experience. I might have been a bit green in the face by the time we landed, but what an amazing and unforgettable trip. What adventures do you want to experience? There are countless options, and the choice is all yours!

> **Exercise**
>
> If you don't already have one, create a bucket list with all the things you'd like to see or do in the next ten years and beyond. What things are you passionate about that you keep talking about but haven't done anything about yet? Put them on your bucket list. Have some fun with this! It is worth asking your friends for inspiration too: what's the best thing they have ever done? Or the craziest thing they ever did to push their boundaries, which they are most proud of?
>
> Once you have created your bucket list, pick the one item you are most excited about, and start taking some action. If you've always wanted to travel to South America, for example, get some inspiring holiday brochures today, decide when and where you want to go, and figure out how much money you need to save each month to make it happen. Even if your financial situation means it will take you fifteen months to get the money together, stop just talking about it and get the ball rolling now!

Closing note

In my private life, dealing with pending actions in a 'do it now' fashion is not something I am very good at. I am not sure why – maybe because I am trying to do too many things, maybe because I am less disciplined with personal affairs than business matters, or possibly because I just can't be bothered, I really don't know. But what I do know is that when I take it on, and 'do it now' for everything that comes up, the resulting clean slate is incredibly liberating and feels fantastic. Even as I am writing this chapter I have a to-do pile next to me which requires my attention at some point. On top of the pile is a letter from the dentist (from three months ago, no less), requesting that I book my yearly check-up. So I finally made the call just now – it took all of two minutes!

When it comes to doing the things I enjoy doing but never find time for, things look a lot better. The first time I wrote a bucket list in my late twenties, it was very long and seemingly impossible. It has since inspired many of my actions as well as numerous travel adventures. I've had an amazing time exploring the world and challenging my limits, and with a bucket list that is a lot shorter now, I have a huge bank of great memories of things I've done with others and on my own. It makes me sad though when I speak to people about all the things I've done and hear them getting all excited, only to explain to me in the very next sentence why they would never be able to make their own dreams a reality. Why not, I say? The world is your oyster! So I invite you to take it on and play your game called life full out. Remember, the only person that can hold you back is yourself. If you truly want something and go for it, you become unstoppable, no matter how many challenges you are faced with. So start making your big dreams a reality – today!

8ᵀᴴ SECRET: SIMPLIFY YOUR LIFE

*Besides the noble art of getting things done,
there is a nobler art of leaving things undone.
The wisdom of life consists in the elimination of non-essentials.*

Lin Yutang (writer, 1895–1976)

What does it mean to 'simplify your life'?

In 2015, the Gallup World Poll conducted a survey in 148 countries to find out which had the happiest citizens.[18] Five key parameters were used to determine the 'Positive Experience Index':

- Feeling well-rested
- Laughing and smiling
- Experiencing enjoyment
- Feeling respected
- Learning or doing something interesting

Using this as the basis for measuring happiness, the results were striking, as they showed that the people of the poorest countries were the happiest, with Paraguay, Colombia, Ecuador and Guatemala at the top of the list. Why is that? Maybe because there is something very powerful in focusing on the simple things in life and appreciating the beauty of an uncluttered life. Simplifying your life means eliminating as many unnecessary distractions as possible.

There are many different forms of distractions. Physical possessions are the most obvious. Some spiritual teachers argue that simplifying your life is best done in poor man's shoes, that wealth, in itself, is too much of a complication to find true happiness and fulfilment. The above study may well be proof of that. That said, I haven't come across many wealthy teachers who give away all their money and possessions to find a place of happiness. But I do believe there is truth in the assertion that a large number of possessions can be a distraction, which can impact happiness. It seems logical that the more things we have, the more time we have to spend looking after them.

Other forms of distractions might be less obvious, but amount to just as much clutter as physical possessions. These include continuous sensory and information overloads, through all the different media surrounding us. How often during the day are you not exposed to any type of media, be it the phone, tablet, computer, newspaper, magazine, radio or TV? When I commute into central London I hardly ever see anyone looking out of the window these days – everyone is keeping busy with some form of media (me included!). We are so used to being occupied with something all day, every day, that it has become normal for us to fill almost every minute with some form of activity. Do you ever allow yourself to sit down and simply 'be', merely enjoying your own company for a few minutes? I think such moments are very rare for most of us.

The more your life is filled with activity, information and material things, the harder it becomes to find some calm and quiet time – time to recharge your batteries and reconnect with that elusive place of inner peace. Or in other words, the more cluttered your life is, the harder it becomes to be happy. This chapter looks at how to simplify your life, reducing the 'white noise' and reclaiming some all-important time for yourself. Since different things work for different people, there is a good-sized menu of ideas to choose from, but don't let that become a distraction. Once you have reached the end of the chapter, just pick your favourite ideas and give them a try.

More is better – or is it?

Modern society operates on the premise that more is better. Success is usually measured by the amount of money and number of cars, houses and yachts people possess. The more status symbols owned, and the more expensive and shiny they are, the more successful people are considered to be. However, what are all these people ultimately striving for? Is it not their aim in life to find happiness and fulfilment? I am sure that no matter what anyone is after, the reason they are going after it is because they believe it will make them happy. That can only mean one thing: the ultimate measure of success is not wealth and possessions, but how much happiness is experienced on a daily basis.

I like the following quote by an unknown author: "The richest person is not the one who has the most but the one who needs the least." Closing the gap between what you have and what you want – which is often what people think is the way to happiness – is not really about getting more stuff, but about needing less. Have you noticed that we seldom seem to reach a point where we have everything we want and there is absolutely nothing else we need? There is always something 'more and better' out there to go after – perhaps we are just not meant to stay still. Yet the secret is to enjoy what you have, moment by moment. Reclaim some time for yourself. Less really is more!

> **Exercise**
>
> It's time to practise some 'me-time'. Put your book or mobile device away, and spend a couple of minutes just enjoying your own company. Allow yourself to sit comfortably and just 'be', with nothing to do and nowhere to get to. If you are out and about, listen for the peace and quiet underneath all the hustle and bustle. Can you hear it, the calmness that is hidden just below the surface of all the noise around you? Can you feel the sense of peace? Maybe there is even a sense of contentment creeping in, too?
>
> Give yourself a few minutes to explore and listen to the quiet around you and inside you. Trust yourself: it is there. Luxuriate in the idea that, for a few minutes, there is nothing you have to do and nowhere you have to be. And as you hold these thoughts, remember that it does not take years of practice to find a place of calmness and happiness within you. You can give yourself permission at any moment to cut out all distractions and just 'be'.

Declutter your mind

Simplifying your life starts with a clear mind – one that can focus on what is essential, without getting sidetracked by unnecessary background noise. But how do we declutter the mind? We have already covered the mental decluttering practice of 'do it now' in the previous chapter. There are other useful techniques to help keep your mind free of unnecessary distractions, which are worth mentioning here:

- **Meditate to quieten the mind.** Meditation is a simple, yet very powerful practice to quieten the mind and it can be done anytime, anywhere. You don't need to be sitting in a lotus position on a straw mat and be surrounded by lovely sounds and smells to meditate; you can use meditation right now, wherever you are. Simply focus on your breathing, noticing how you breathe in and out. Because the mind can only centre on one thought at a time, the focus on your breath will quieten down the internal chatter in your head about whatever it is that has been occupying your mind.

- **Keep things in perspective.** We can occasionally get completely carried away with little upsets and incidents, simply because we are right in the middle of them and cannot see the bigger picture. In such moments, it can help to ask yourself: "Will I remember this in six months' time?" If the answer is no, then it is probably not worth losing sleep over it. Focus on what is important and let little niggles go.

- **Do one thing at a time.** We can get really stressed sometimes by trying to do too many things at once. We think it saves time, but it often just means that we cannot enjoy any of the tasks at hand. Doing multiple things simultaneously doesn't allow us to focus properly on any one activity, which can easily lead to a distracted mind, slowing us down and making us inefficient. When doing just one thing at a time, it is possible to truly embrace the task and practise 'meditation in motion'. All of a sudden, even the most mundane activity, such as vacuuming the floor or mowing the lawn, becomes enjoyable – and it gets done a lot quicker, too.

- **Be more selective with the daily news.** The amount of negative news we are exposed to each day through newspapers, TV, the internet, Twitter and other social media is a big contributor to cluttered minds. Choose carefully how much of your precious time you want to spend informing yourself about daily events, as they do affect how you think. How uplifting can it be to read about murders and other terrible things happening in the world? The more negative news you watch or hear, the more likely it is for you to have negative thoughts, simply by thinking about what you have just seen or read. To be informed about what is happening in the world, consider choosing just one newspaper, website or app that can provide you with the key news of the day within a few minutes – then put it away and focus on more uplifting activities.

Example

I once decided to take this last point to the extreme and cut out all news sources for an entire year. I did not watch TV or listen to the radio, I did not read any newspapers and did not even check my phone or the internet for daily news updates. I was tired of all the negative news and wanted to know what it would feel like to not be exposed to any of it for a year. I had some concerns, of course, that I might miss out on important events, but any vital headlines always found their way to me. I think it is virtually impossible to avoid news exposure completely, certainly if you live or work in a city like London. Not reading the news, however, freed up a lot of time. Not being bombarded with negative headlines first thing in the morning also made it much easier to start the day on a happy note and then stay in a positive frame of mind throughout the day. It was a very enjoyable experiment and a great year, and I did not feel that I was missing out on anything at all. Since then, I have become very selective about where I get my news from and how much time I spend reading up on the day's events. I feel it has made my days a lot less cluttered and much more peaceful.

Declutter your home and work environment

The concept of simplifying your life becomes most visible when looking at your environment. It means keeping things as uncluttered and functional as possible, while at the same time still being comfortable. It starts with simple things like keeping your work and living environment tidy, keeping any dust collecting knick-knacks to a minimum, and having a regular clear out of things that are unwanted or unused. Physical decluttering is key to a peaceful life and a calm mind. Never underestimate the impact of a messy environment on the brain! From a Law of Attraction perspective, a cluttered environment can dilute your power as a deliberate creator, because your focus gets distracted by too many things. Letting go of things that are no longer relevant to your current experience releases old energy and makes room for the new.

If you find it difficult to get rid of things – be it by throwing them away, giving them to charity or selling them – get a few boxes and put any items away that have been collecting dust, unless they make you feel good when you look at them. Be honest with yourself. If you are worried that you might need some of these items in the future, number the boxes and keep a simple log where you can note down what you have put into each box, to make it easy to retrieve anything if required. Chances are, there will be one or two items that you need, a few months down the line – and they will probably be at the bottom of the box that is the hardest to reach in storage. But it is well worth getting things out of the way now and feeling that sense of space again.

> **Exercise**
>
> Look around your home and find ten things that are on display or just lying around which you don't need any longer. Decide to give them to charity, sell them on eBay, or throw them away today, and notice how much lighter you will feel.

Feng Shui

One great technique to help simplify your home and work environment is Feng Shui. Feng Shui is defined as 'the Chinese practice of creating harmonious surroundings that enhance the balance of Yin and Yang'.[19] It is a philosophy that aims to optimise the energy flow of your environment. It suggests that the right positions, along with using the right shapes, colours, layouts and designs, can make the energy flow better and inspire your creative powers to work to their maximum capacity. A home or work environment that is aligned with some basic Feng Shui principles naturally feels good. It will set an excellent foundation in your endeavours to live a happy and well balanced life, day after day.

Feng Shui is a very elaborate art form that requires years of study. Hiring a Feng Shui expert can be expensive, but there are some basic tips that are easy to implement:

- **Trust your instincts.** You might not be aware of it, but your instincts are likely to tell you already how well the energy flows in your environment. In which rooms in your home do you like to spend most of your time and which do you usually avoid? If you really enjoy spending time in your kitchen, but hardly use your family room, it suggests that your family room is in need of some attention and Feng Shui improvements, while the kitchen is probably in pretty good shape.

- **Remove clutter.** Here it is again, the importance of removing distractions or 'energy disturbances' in the form of physical clutter. Decluttering is absolutely essential from a Feng Shui perspective. The first thing to start with – as any Feng Shui expert will tell you – is to get rid of anything you don't use and don't love. It really is amazing what a difference an uncluttered room can make and how it instantly becomes more inviting.

- **Allow air and light to enrich your house.** Good air and light in your home are the next key ingredients, as they are essential for good Feng Shui energy. Aim to allow as much natural light in through your windows as possible, by keeping heavy curtains to a minimum – and open your windows regularly, to get some fresh air.

- **Decorate to support the room's function.** Each room in your home has a purpose. The bedrooms and bathroom are there for relaxation, while the kitchen, family room and home office are very active spaces. Calm environments are best supported with deep and soft colours, while more active rooms should be dominated by strong, vibrant colours and bright lights. The TV, exercise equipment and office items are good examples of active energy that should be kept away from the bedroom. For your home to feel comfortable it is important to keep the calm energy (Yin) and active energy (Yang) well balanced and represented appropriately in each room, according to the room's function.

- **Put your furniture where you feel most comfortable.** When you move into a new home, you are likely to furnish it first and then, over time, pick your favourite places to sit and relax. At least that is how most of us usually do it. When we bought our current house, we decided to take a different approach. We invited a Feng Shui expert to come around with a little chair on wheels, before moving in. We spent a few hours exploring the space of each room and finding the best positions. It turned out that the place where we originally wanted to put the TV was in fact the most comfortable place to sit and the one with the best view. So we made quite a few changes to our original plans, positioning the sofas, chairs and beds in line with where it felt best to be – and then arranging all the other furniture around them. What a difference it made! But the most interesting thing was that it all intuitively made sense. Certain positions in the room did naturally feel better than others, even without the expert having to confirm it.

> **Exercise**
>
> Give it a try yourself. Let's say you don't enjoy spending time in your home office. Get a chair (ideally with wheels) and sit in different positions of the room, facing the window, then facing the door. Where does it feel best to get some work done? Each room has certain positions that function better than others. When it comes to your workspace, it is usually best to sit facing the door, with any windows on your side, if possible. This allows you to see when someone comes in, which means that your primal instincts of wanting to be safe and in control are satisfied, while still enjoying the view out of the window.

These tips only touch the surface of the intricacies of Feng Shui, of course, but I think they can still make a significant difference in how you feel about your home and work environment. It really doesn't have to cost much to Feng Shui your home.

Living a simple life

So what does living a simple life look like day to day? We have already explored the most important ingredient: declutter, declutter, and then declutter some more. Clear your environment on a regular basis of things you don't need any longer, and clear your mind from the sensory and information overloads of today's world. Here are some additional suggestions of things to try, to experience the joys of a simple life:

- **Make time for what is important to you and what you enjoy doing.** Stop rushing from one thing to the next, all day long. Things that are important to you should feature at the top of your priority list and get the time they deserve in your busy schedule. Health and wellbeing are prime examples of things that are very important, but, usually, take second (or ninth or tenth) place in our busy lives. You don't need a dog to go for a nice brisk walk or a run first thing in the morning before going to work – and your body will thank you for it. Don't confine me-time to the weekend. Use your creativity and imagination to free up time during the week to do something for yourself that you enjoy.

- **Manage your to-do list.** There is nothing more frustrating and stressful than having a completely overwhelming to-do list that never gets any shorter. Go through your list and identify what is really important, and what is not. What things can you drop from the list altogether, rather than keep ignoring them for weeks and weeks, making yourself feel guilty? Give yourself permission not to do certain things. When I took this on, I went through my eternally oversized to-do pile and realised that I had a lot of documents that I had been meaning to read for months, such as 'Variations to your bank account T&Cs', and other such exciting materials. I decided to be honest with myself and admit that I would never read these anyway. It instantly reduced my paper pile by about two thirds. I would also recommend that you commit to a manageable number of to do items per day, say the three that are most on your mind, particularly if your days are very busy already. Focus on getting those done, rather than trying to do fifteen things and feeling too overwhelmed to do any. Pat yourself on the back when they are done and enjoy the sense of achievement!

- **Slow down.** Breathe, take regular breaks and focus on enjoying every task at hand. Because life is not happening once your tasks are done; your tasks and other things that keep you busy <u>are</u> your life! And every now and then, just enjoy doing nothing. Stop thinking that you need to fill every minute of the day with something to do – and instead, allow yourself to just 'be'.

- **A tip for your work environment, specifically.** If you have a lot of meetings throughout the day, don't schedule them back to back. Instead, leave some time for yourself to recharge and mentally prepare for the next meeting. Even just five minutes can make a big difference. I have worked with many different companies and it is very common to see people rushing from meeting to meeting without getting anything done (and then working overtime in the evening as a result). It was also quite shocking to see how often people would sit in a meeting without any preparation and with no clarity on the objectives of the discussion – they were not very productive meetings, to say the least. When I wear the hat of a meeting facilitator, a key role I play at the start of a meeting is to ensure the meeting participants are clear and in agreement on the purpose of the meeting, as well as what a good outcome looks like. If you can walk into each meeting calm and centred, because you just had a nice quick breather and time to think about the purpose and desired outcomes of the meeting, you are bound to save yourself (and every other meeting attendee) time, by making the meeting more focused and productive. This will help to make it worthwhile for everyone involved, and it might even eliminate the need for further meetings on the same topic.

> **Exercise**
>
> Pick your favourite three ideas from this chapter and, for three days over the coming week, experiment with each one as the 'theme for the day'. Observe how you feel while exploring them and what difference they make in your day.

Closing note

Life is a bit like a backpacking holiday: the less stuff you carry with you, the lighter and less restricted you feel, and the more you can enjoy the trip. When I took time out from the corporate world in 2007 to start my travel adventures around the world, I sold nearly all my possessions. I wanted to experience the freedom of not being attached to anything: no house I'd have to come back to and no furniture to worry about. However, there were still a few things I thought I could not live without. I desperately tried to squeeze them all in, which resulted in a backpack weighing a whopping 30kg! It was not a very pleasant experience to travel even very short distances, to say the least. I learned my lesson quickly and got the weight down to 18kg. For a year, my whole life was in that backpack and it turned out that 18kg of 'stuff' was really all I needed. It was a magical experience to live the simple life and explore other cultures around the world, just me and my backpack. It seems we really need very little when it comes down to it.

Of course, I am not suggesting that you get rid of all your belongings and travel around the world (although I can highly recommend it!). But I do invite you to take a look at the backpack that you carry around with you, right now. Is your life as uncluttered as you would like it to be? And do you spend your time on what is important to you? If your backpack is too heavy for your liking, experiment with the various ideas in this chapter and see what difference they make to your stress levels and general wellbeing. Then pick the suggestions that work best for you and integrate them into your everyday routine. And remember: less is more!

9TH SECRET:
NURTURE YOUR BODY, MIND AND SOUL

We are not human beings having a spiritual experience.
We are spiritual beings having a human experience.

Pierre Teilhard de Chardin (French philosopher, 1881–1955)

What does it mean to 'nurture your body, mind and soul'?

You are a three-part being: you have a body, a mind and a soul. The body is the physical part of you which enables you to feel, taste, smell, see and hear what is happening around you. It also enables you to move about and communicate with the world through your mouth, your hands, your facial expressions and your body language. Your mind enables you to prioritise and process all the information you receive through the different sensory organs of your body, and give it some meaning. It is the part that analyses and questions, allows you to imagine and daydream, or worry and get stressed out. Your soul is the oldest and wisest part of you, your higher self and pure life force that is eternal and can't be destroyed. It is where your inner child lives, as mentioned in Secret 2 'Be in the moment'. The soul is the source of your passions and your purpose, and your emotions are your soul's way to communicate with you: if you feel positive emotions like joy and appreciation you are in alignment with your soul and eternal being; if you feel negative emotions such as anger or jealousy you are not.

Nurturing your body, mind and soul means looking after all three parts of your being. Your body needs nourishment, some exercise and care. Your mind requires stimulation, intellectually and creatively, and needs to be used on a regular basis like a muscle, to stay active. And your soul's nourishment consists of love and attention, not just from the people that are important to you but even more so from yourself. Nurturing all three parts of your self is absolutely essential for your general wellbeing, and it is not possible to reach a sustainable state of happiness without all three parts of your being well looked after and nourished.

Nurturing your body

Healthy, balanced nutrition and some regular exercise are well-known key factors to general wellbeing and therefore also to happiness. There are many excellent books on the market that cover nutrition and exercise in great detail, and it would go beyond the scope of this book to try to give these topics the necessary attention they deserve. However, there are a few very basic but crucial points that are worth mentioning here on nutrition and exercise.

Key basics on nutrition

- **Drink plenty of water.** Our bodies are made of about 60% water, so if you want to take on just one thing, make sure you drink plenty of water. Aim to drink at least eight glasses of water a day. Keep coffee and any other caffeine-containing drinks to a minimum, as they dehydrate the body, and avoid sugary drinks as much as possible.

- **Have your five-a-day.** Yes I know you know, but it's too important not to mention it here: five portions of fruit and vegetables a day is a great foundation for a healthy diet. Remember that fruit is usually high in sugars, so aim for as many vegetable portions in your five-a-day as possible. And five is not a limit of course – the more the better!

- **Mix your colours.** An easy way to ensure a varied diet is to mix different colour foods, as the colour is an indicator for the type of nutrients the food contains. So the more colourful your plate, the more varied your nutrients intake will be – assuming there are no added colourants in the food, of course (so no, M&Ms are not high in nutrients, just in case you were wondering).

- **Get the right balance of carbohydrates, protein, fat and fibre.** Most of us know that carbohydrates, protein and fibre are good for us, and fat is bad. But is it really? It all comes down to getting the balance right, because even fat plays an important role, in the right quality and quantity.[20]

    - About 60% of your daily calorie intake should come from carbohydrates. Carbohydrates are your body's main source of energy, and are needed for your heart, kidneys, brain and muscles to function properly. For a healthy diet, it's important to choose carbohydrates in their most natural form, such as whole grains, fresh fruit, vegetables, milk and yogurt, rather than processed foods with additives.

    - Protein is essential for the body to build and repair tissue, and is an important building block of bones, muscles, skin, and blood. About 20% of calories should come from protein. Its key role in growth makes it particularly important for children, teenagers and pregnant women. Unlike carbohydrates, the body does not store protein. Protein is primarily found in meats, poultry, fish, cheese, milk, eggs, nuts and beans.

- Despite its bad reputation, <u>fat</u> is important as well, with ideally about 20% of your daily calorie intake coming from it. Fat is needed to absorb certain vitamins (A, D, E and K), provide energy, and provide some protective cushioning for your cells and organs. However, the key is to minimise saturated fats (found in foods like meat, butter, lard, and cream) as well as trans fats (in baked goods, snack foods, fried foods, and margarines), as they increase the risk of heart disease. Instead, replace them by unsaturated fat, found in foods like olive oil, fish, avocados and nuts.

- <u>Fibre</u> is needed to keep the digestive system healthy, but it also helps to prevent heart disease, diabetes, weight gain and some cancers. Fibre is only found in food that comes from plants, i.e. cereals, fruits and vegetables. Meat, fish and dairy products don't contain any fibre. Many people don't get enough fibre: in the UK, most people get about 14g of fibre a day on average, but you should aim for at least 18g a day.

- **Keep sugar and salt to a minimum.** Of course everyone knows that sugar and salt should be kept to a minimum as much as possible. The trick is to be aware of the hidden salts and sugars in food. Hidden sugars are often particularly high in low fat foods, to compensate for loss of flavour. Other sources of high sugar content include non-alcoholic drinks (in the UK, they account for up to 25% of daily intake of added sugar), some breakfast cereals, and alcohol, to mention just the worst culprits. Ready-made meals as well as fresh soups and sauces are usually high in salt, as salt works as a natural preservative.

If you want to keep your salt intake low, it's best to cook food from scratch.

- **Give your food the attention it deserves.** Avoid eating in front of the TV or your computer. I know it is very tempting to eat your lunch in front of your computer if you are busy, or to nibble on some sweet or savoury snacks in front of the TV (I'm guilty as charged too). But if your mind is not fully focused on the food, then your body isn't either, and your body will either digest the food poorly, or you will overeat (I'm sure I didn't just eat the whole ice cream pot, or did I?).

Key basics on exercise

When it comes to exercise, many associate it with the dreadful thought of having to force themselves to go to the gym three times a week, which means they end up doing nothing at all as a result. But it doesn't have to be that way! It's actually quite easy to give your body what it needs to stay healthy in terms of physical activity.

- **Breathe deeply!** Just because we do it automatically and all the time doesn't mean that breathing doesn't deserve some special attention and care. Most of us are very shallow breathers. Try to fit in some deep breaths as often as you can, particularly when you are out and about. Get some fresh air into your lungs – your body will thank you for it!

- **Aim for regular exercise.** Yes you should do some exercise, but it's important you choose something you enjoy doing – there are many other ways to get fit that don't involve buying an expensive gym membership, if you dread going to the gym. Also, it is better to do just a little bit every day than taking on too much once a week. It should be something that makes you feel good and that can help you to de-stress and get rid of negative energy. A twenty minute brisk walk is easy to fit into the day and is a very gentle and effective form of exercise. Just get off a couple of bus stops earlier on your way home and walk the rest, or use your lunch break to explore your surroundings a bit. If you are new to exercise, then yoga is another great place to start as it's a very gentle form of exercise compared to other sports. It is a great all-rounder which combines muscular exercise with stretching, and has the added bonus of being a form of meditation in motion, thus helping to calm and nurture your mind and soul as well.

- **Exercise your eyes.** Our vision is one of those precious things that is taken for granted until it starts to go. Sitting in front of the computer all day long is very strenuous for the eyes. To relax and strengthen your eye muscles, take short breaks for your eyes as often as possible, by looking away from the screen to something at a distance. Refocusing your eyes a few times from something close to something far away strengthens the eye muscles and helps to reduce the strain of staring at a screen for long periods of time.

- **Treat yourself to a massage.** Besides regular exercise I think it's important to pamper yourself on a regular basis. After all, the body you've got is the only one you'll ever have in this life, so it deserves a bit of a special treat every now and then! If getting a massage from your partner or a professional massage therapist is not an option, then just buy a nice smelling massage oil or foot balm and give yourself a relaxing foot massage, possibly combined with a hot bath. From a reflexology perspective, the sole of the foot is a mirror of your body, with over 7,000 nerve endings that correspond to every part within your body, so the whole body will benefit when you massage your feet.

We are meant to thrive and experience wellbeing. Looking after your body is a very important part of looking after yourself, and forms a key part of the foundation for a happy, healthy and fulfilling life.

> **Exercise**
>
> Experiment with the above suggestions on nutrition and exercise for the next few days, and see what a difference they make to your energy levels. Looking after your body doesn't take much time and effort, but it will make all the difference in how you feel and the energy you've got!

Nurturing your mind

Your thoughts play a key role in how life occurs to you. They decide whether to interpret an experience as positive or negative, and they are a main driver for your general wellbeing. Or in other words: the quality of your life is determined by the quality of your thoughts. It is therefore absolutely essential to have a healthy and well nurtured mind. And just as the body needs healthy food and regular exercise, the mind needs positive stimulation in order to thrive. It is like a muscle; it needs to be used and challenged, otherwise it starts to disengage and shrivel. Positive stimulation comes in all shapes and sizes, and varies greatly based on personal interests. Some people enjoy creative activity like painting or doing handicraft, while others prefer the more intellectual stimulation they can get through reading a good book, doing crossword puzzles or a home study course.

Whatever the activity, it's all about keeping the mind active and engaged with something you enjoy doing. Rediscover some of your passions from the past, or try something new. If you like intellectual stimulation, learn to play chess, practise your Sudoku skills, or read an interesting book. If you prefer creative stimulation, why not try painting, knitting, gardening or pottery? The options are endless. And in addition to whatever it is you choose, consider complementing it with meditation and affirmations, to nourish your mind with positive and relaxing messages.

Meditation

Meditation has been mentioned a few times throughout this book already as a powerful technique to get present to the here and now, and switch off any white noise or negative internal dialogue in your head. Meditation helps to rebalance and rejuvenate your mind, and helps you feel peaceful and grounded. Meditating doesn't have to be a complicated process. One of the best and most powerful ways to meditate is to simply focus on your breathing, as mentioned in Secret 2 'Be in the moment'. Just fifteen minutes of conscious breathing will provide a calming sense of groundedness, and is a great way to start or end a day. Here are a few things to keep in mind to make your meditation as effective as possible:

- **Choose a simple focus.** Whatever you use as your focus of meditation, whether it is your breath, a mantra (a word, sound or short sentence), a mental picture (e.g. a rose or a candle), or whatever else you are inspired by, choose something simple. It is easier to stay focused on a simple thought.

- **Set a daily 'meditation time'.** Find a time that works for you and stick to that time slot as much as possible. This will make it easier to build up a routine.

- **Avoid any distractions.** Make sure you don't get disturbed during your meditation. Switch off your phone and block the time in your calendar. Let the people around you know that you are about to meditate and don't want to be disturbed. There is nothing more distracting than to constantly have to worry that someone might come and interrupt you while meditating.

- **Be comfortable.** Make sure you sit in a position that you can stay in for the duration of the meditation. If you have back or knee problems, you will probably be more comfortable sitting in an upright chair than on the floor or a meditation stool.

- **Keep it short.** Fifteen minutes is a good duration for a daily meditation, and will make a noticeable difference to your frame of mind and stress levels. Anything longer is often difficult to fit into a daily routine.

There are many other ways to nurture your mind than meditation of course, but when I have a bad day and feel deflated, and not even the best music seems to be able to cheer me up, I find meditation a great place of last resort. It softens the negative thoughts and emotions I'm experiencing, and allows me to find my place of balance and groundedness again.

Affirmations

Providing your mind with positive messages throughout the day is another great way to nourish your mind. Using positive affirmations, as explained in Part 1 of the book under the chapter 'The power of the underlying belief system', is a very easy and effective way to do so. All it takes is a simple affirmation like 'I love my life!' or 'I feel great!' said to yourself a few times throughout the day, and it will give you a positive mental boost right away. What you say to yourself all day long can lift you up or drag you down – it's completely your choice and in your control. Nobody has as much power over you as you do to make your life very joyful or very miserable. Choose to nourish your mind with positive messages, and leverage the power of affirmations to do so.

Stress management

Stress is probably one of the biggest sources for ailments in today's modern society, and is very much a creation of the human mind. Stress doesn't exist anywhere else in nature the way the human society has managed to build it into its daily fabric. And since stress is probably one of the most likely reasons keeping you from taking the time to nurture your body, mind and soul, it is worth mentioning stress management here. There is an excellent little story that summarises the nature of stress very well:

A lecturer, when explaining stress management to an audience, raised a glass of water and asked, "How heavy is this glass of water?" Answers called out ranged from 20g to 500g. The lecturer replied, "The absolute weight doesn't matter. It depends on how long you try to hold it. If I hold it for a minute, that's not a problem. If I hold it for an hour, I'll have an ache in my right arm. If I hold it for a day, you'll have to call an ambulance. In each case, it's the same weight, but the longer I hold it, the heavier it becomes." He continued, "And that's the way it is with stress management. If we carry our burdens all the time, sooner or later, as the burden becomes increasingly heavy, we won't be able to carry on. As with the glass of water, you have to put it down for a while and rest before holding it again. When we're refreshed, we can carry on with the burden. So, before you return home tonight, put the burden of work down. Don't carry it home. You can pick it up tomorrow.

Whatever burden you're carrying now, let it down for a moment."
(Author unknown)

So, make sure you take regular breaks, and leave your work-related stresses at work at the end of the day. I find it quite helpful to visualise putting all my work-related worries into a little cabinet by my desk and locking them away with a key before I go home – that way I know they will still be there the next morning, which feels strangely reassuring because it means I don't have to worry about them overnight. It allows me to get a good night's sleep, and deal with it all much more effectively the next morning. However you do it, make sure you properly switch off in the evening; do something that makes you feel good. It's time well spent and will help relax your mind, which in turn will make any challenges much more manageable.

> **Exercise**
>
> What do you enjoy doing to nourish your mind? Write down your top three favourite activities that fall into the creative or intellectual category to stimulate or relax your mind, and make time this week to give at least one of them a go!

Nurturing your soul

The soul is the oldest and wisest part of you, the part that doesn't die when your body and mind find their final resting place. It could be described as your life force or life energy, and while most people can't see the soul (unless you are able to see auras), it's what you sense instinctively when you meet someone. You might call it charisma: it's what lights up the room when some people enter before they even say a word, because of their strong energy field. It is the part of you that knows that you are whole, complete and perfect exactly the way you are.

So how do you nurture the soul? It is quite self-explanatory how to take care of the body and the mind. Nurturing the soul is a lot less tangible, but you will know how well it is nurtured by how you feel: the happier and more at peace you are, the better your soul is nurtured. With the foundation of a healthy and balanced body and mind in place, it all becomes a matter of the heart: nourish your soul by doing things that make your heart sing. Many of the ideas mentioned in this book fall into this category. There are just a few additional activities I'd like to mention here which work particularly well to nurture the soul. Be open minded about what follows – if you are not very spiritual, it might push your boundaries a bit.

Tune in with your life force

I find it helpful to remind myself from time to time that I'm a spiritual being in a human body, that there is more to me than just my physical shell. Why? Because it puts everything in perspective, and reminds me to not get upset about insignificant things like something someone said in the heat of an argument. It's like looking at the world from 30,000 feet – you can see the bigger picture much better. When I tune in with my life force, I feel grounded and uplifted at the same time, ready to take on the world.

To tune in with your life force, sit quietly with your eyes closed, and start by focusing on the physical boundaries of your body. Where does your body end, and where do your surroundings start? Once you are fully aware of your body, start to reach out and see if you can sense the part of you that is there beyond your physical boundary. It's the part of you that would be described as your energy field, your aura, which is not constrained by the physical limits of the body. Feel its presence, its warmth and light, and tune into it. Feel how it extends beyond your body. Give yourself a few minutes, and imagine yourself as a beacon of light which fills its surroundings with love and warmth. And then, all of a sudden, it doesn't just feel like you're imagining it. That's when you know you are tuned in with your life force. Feel how its power and presence fills the room, and allow yourself to become fully aware of the magnificence of your life force, your soul.

This is a great exercise to remind yourself that you are more than a physical body. Do you ever get goosebumps when you hear or do something that truly resonates with you? This is what this exercise does to me. I am a spiritual adventurer, and while I have read many spiritual books and done courses to explore the non-physical (like practising out-of-body experiences), I don't consider myself an expert in the spiritual realm. Ultimately, I mostly just follow my intuition as much as possible, and would encourage you to do the same. When I do the above exercise, with my eyes closed, it's like the sun comes out from behind a bank of clouds and it becomes very bright in front of my eyelids. I can feel that the exercise nourishes my soul and re-energises my life force, which brightens up my aura and is what I can see with my eyes closed. And I feel fantastic as a result, happy and full of energy. Give it a try, and see if you can tune in to your life force. Don't worry though if it doesn't work for you – it is just one of many ways to nurture your soul.

Reconnect with your inner child

I have already mentioned this technique in Secret 2 'Be in the moment'. Reconnecting with your inner child is a great way to tune in with your soul and nourish it. If you tried to tune in with your inner child while reading Secret 2, but you either couldn't find it or the child didn't want to come near you, try to understand what is pushing your child away. What do you need to do to gain the child's trust and closeness again? Chances are, the child feels neglected because you've been busy for years without giving it any attention. After all, you most likely didn't even know it existed! Spending a few minutes with him or her every day for a week or two is all that is needed to reconnect. You will feel the difference when you and your inner child have fully bonded again – you will feel uplifted and full of energy. That's what being tuned in with your soul feels like.

Example

I have to admit that life's busy-ness does get the better of me at times, and the first thing that usually suffers is the nurturing of my soul and inner child. As I am writing this chapter, our little daughter is eleven months old, and she has been keeping me very busy ever since she was born. I absolutely adore our cheeky little monkey, and I know my inner child totally adores her too, but it is probably fair to say that I have neglected myself and my inner child quite a bit while learning the ins and outs of looking after a demanding little person full of beans. So when I closed my eyes one evening to reconnect with my inner child after several months of not tuning in, I couldn't find her at first. It was only after a few minutes that I saw an image of her in the nursery, curled up next to our baby girl and watching over her. My inner child had fully bonded with our daughter, but she had distanced herself from me. It took a little coaxing before she dropped her shyness and suspicion and gave me a hug. And it felt so good! Even though it all just happened in my imagination, while lying on my bed with my eyes closed, it felt like I had just found a part of me again that I had lost without even knowing it.

Tuning in with your inner child is a very important and effective way to nurture your soul, as it personifies your subconscious. So if you haven't tried it yet, I invite you to give it a try now and see for yourself what your inner child might have in store for you. Worst case, it doesn't work. But if it does work for you, you have just found a very powerful way to nourish your soul. Allow yourself to be blown away by the creativity, energy and great sense of humour of your inner child when you give it your love and attention!

Tai Chi

I am well aware that I am probably asking quite a lot from some readers to tune in with their life force or their inner child. If you are struggling with these spiritual concepts, then Tai Chi is a more down to earth alternative to nurture your soul. Originally developed as a form of martial arts in the thirteenth century, Tai Chi is a very popular Chinese tradition which is practised around the world today. It consists of a series of gentle movements performed in a slow, focused manner that are accompanied by deep breathing. As such, it combines meditation with light exercise, and is a fantastic way to nurture body, mind and soul all at the same time. It works with the energy meridians of the body to bring the energy flow into alignment and improve the flow of Qi energy. Just fifteen minutes a day, ideally in the morning, can give you some excellent grounding and energy for the day ahead. Practising Tai Chi on a regular basis helps to reduce stress by relaxing the body and helping to keep the mind calm and focused. It also improves body balance and flexibility, and increases muscle strength in the legs. So if you are not the type that likes to sit still to meditate, then Tai Chi might be worth a try.

Other ways to nurture your soul

There are of course many other ways to nourish your soul. Ultimately, only you know what speaks to you at your most fundamental level. What is it that makes your heart sing? Here are some ideas that can help to reignite the life force and nurture your soul:

- **Spend time in nature.** There is something very healing about spending time in nature. Nature speaks to the soul and is very soothing in today's busy world. So spend time in nature as often as you can.
- **Find and feed your passions.** Step out of your daily routine and rediscover the adventurous side of you – do something for yourself that makes you feel good and makes your heart sing.
- **Make music part of your life.** Singing your favourite songs, or listening to your favourite tracks, is very powerful and uplifting. Music is great for the soul.
- **Spend some time on your own.** Enjoy your own company. Get to know yourself, and learn to appreciate your uniqueness.
- **Meditate and find your inner place of peace.** Meditation doesn't just nurture the mind – it benefits body, mind and soul. Spending even just five minutes a day to listen within and reconnecting with our true self is balm for the soul.
- **Switch off your brain, and let your heart lead the way.** Dance in the rain, watch a sunrise, make love outdoors, swim naked – let go of society's constraints and allow yourself to enjoy life to the fullest. Be daring, step out of your comfort zone, and have some fun!

Exercise

It's time to make some all-important time for yourself and nurture your soul. Pick one idea from this section that particularly spoke to you or choose something else that makes your heart sing, and make some time for it this week!

Aligning body, mind and soul: the power of self-healing

So you now know how to nurture your body, mind and soul. But why is it so important to look after all three parts of your being? How do they interact with each other? And more specifically, how do the mind and soul influence the body?

How illnesses are caused by negative thought patterns

Our bodies are absolutely amazing. Scientists are estimating that a human body consists of approximately ten trillion cells (that's 10,000,000,000,000 cells!). Every single one of these cells knows exactly what it is supposed to be doing, and – unless it is damaged – does it successfully every day. Most cells in the body also regenerate themselves: skin cells regenerate after about two to three weeks, red blood cells live for about four months, and a bone takes up to ten years to replace all of its cells. But here is the really interesting thing: our cells take on board our beliefs and thought patterns, and pass on their 'memory' from one generation of cells to the next. That's why even after most of your cells have been replaced you are still you – you look the same, feel the same, and still have all the same memories. It also means that despite the regeneration of cells, negative thought patterns stick around and can translate into energy blockages over time, which eventually become illnesses.

In other words, your mind and soul influence your body, and being out of balance can cause health issues. Illnesses usually have a psychological root cause, and it is well worth listening to your body and responding to its messages, because that's what most health problems are – a message from your body. Louise Hay, spiritual author and teacher, has written an all-time classic and worldwide bestseller called *You Can Heal Your Life*.[21] At the back of her book,

Louise Hay put together a list of illnesses, and linked them to their psychological root cause (i.e. the thought pattern that caused the illness). She also provides affirmations for each illness to help change the negative underlying beliefs. I have used this reference table many times over the years to look up symptoms and ailments that were mentioned to me by my coaching clients, from toothache to infections, skin rashes and hair loss. It still amazes me how Louise Hay was able to create this list – very powerful!

Example

While I was supporting a large transformation project with a UK company, I was working closely with one senior manager in particular, who was suffering from a chronic case of dry cough. He was leading one of the transformation workstreams, and it seemed that his cough always got worse during our weekly project conference calls with the team. Looking up 'coughing' in Louise Hay's book, it said: "A desire to bark at the world: See me! Listen to me!", and the affirmation it suggested was: 'I am noticed and appreciated in the most positive ways. I am loved'. The manager was quite insecure, and felt rather overwhelmed in his new role of a business change leader. The coughing was his subconscious way of getting people's attention so that they would listen to him. We worked on his confidence over the following weeks and months, and by the time the project came to an end he was completely transformed. He had become a confident leader and manager, and his cough had completely disappeared and was long forgotten. After all, his demeanour and leadership style demanded attention now, so the cough's message of 'See me! Listen to me!' had become superfluous.

Using Qigong for self-healing

While minor ailments like the ones mentioned above can quite easily be addressed with affirmations to help reprogramme the negative thought patterns, I have personally found that it is usually not enough to deal with major illnesses. However, the principle remains the same: self-healing occurs when body, mind and soul are fully aligned, and any energy blockages are removed. Qigong is a Far Eastern healing practice and a very powerful technique to nurture body, mind and soul. 'Qi' means life force, while 'Gong' stands for 'accomplishment or skill that is cultivated through steady practice'. Together, Qigong loosely translates as 'looking after your life force through regular practice'.[22] It is a technique which combines breathing, gentle movement and meditation to cleanse and strengthen the life energy. As such, Qigong is another form of meditation in motion, but unlike Tai Chi it is specifically focused on healing the body.

The underlying philosophy of Qigong is that all ailments and illnesses are caused by some form of energy blockages in the body, and by removing these energy blockages it is possible to heal even the most severe illnesses. Its simple but highly effective exercises focus on reinstating the natural energy balance of our being, or in other words, bringing body, mind and soul back into alignment. It is astounding to see the effects of Qigong in healing pains and illnesses, including conditions declared incurable by modern science, such as certain forms of cancer.

There are over 7,000 different types of Qigong that are officially recognised and practised in China. I am most familiar with Spring Forest Qigong (www.springforestqigong.com), developed by Master Chunyi Lin who is based in the US. I use some of the very basic exercises of Spring Forest Qigong to keep my body in a relaxed, energised and healthy state, which sets the foundation for a happy and fulfilled life. There are numerous accounts of Master Chunyi Lin working with cancer patients around the world who completely recovered within a few months, simply by removing certain energy blockages through a combination of hours (and hours!) of specific Qigong exercises for the body and the mind, healthy nutrition, and some supportive healing from Chunyi. The self-healing powers of our bodies are truly incredible, if we know how to tap into them.

Closing note

The body's self-healing power is just one example of what is possible when body, mind and soul are fully aligned and pulling in the same direction. And by the same token, severe illnesses show what happens when that alignment is missing, when we are neglecting one or more parts of our three-part being. So make sure you take the time to nurture your body, mind and soul. When you nurture all three parts of your being, you will notice quickly how much more energy you have. You are also likely to need less sleep, as the soul does not need as much time to recover from the hardships of being in the body as it might have done before. When body, mind and soul are fully aligned and have a common purpose, the amazing person you are really starts to show, and you become virtually unstoppable. It's time to find out what you are capable of when all three parts of you are fully nurtured and in alignment!

10TH SECRET: APPRECIATE WHAT YOU HAVE

*A beautiful day begins with a beautiful mindset.
When you wake up, take a second to think
about what a privilege it is to simply be alive and healthy.
The moment you start acting like life is a blessing,
I assure you it will start to feel like one.*

Author unknown

The power of appreciation

If there was such a thing as a shortcut to finding happiness, it would be to appreciate what you have. In one study, a group of people were asked to keep a gratitude journal for a week, writing down three things they were grateful for every day. And even though the exercise only lasted a week, the participants were happier and less depressed than at the outset of the study, not just immediately after the exercise but one, three and even six months after the seven-day exercise. Another study, which used a daily gratitude journal over a ten-week period, resulted in the participants feeling more joyful, more interested and energetic, and experiencing fewer health problems. Gratitude can reduce blood pressure, lower stress hormones, give you a stronger immune system, and generally makes you happier. Truly astounding! This shows that a simple exercise like writing a gratitude journal can have a profound and lasting impact on your happiness, right away.

But before you can truly appreciate something, you first have to realise that you have it. Are you aware of the amazing relationships you have in your life, and how much the people around you love and care about you? Are you aware of the skills and talents you possess, and all the beautiful memories you have accumulated throughout your life so far? And then of course there are all the physical possessions, conveniences and luxuries in your life that make it more enjoyable. Do you remind yourself occasionally that not everyone in the world has access to a hot shower and a Starbucks coffee in the morning? It is a very powerful exercise to get fully present to everything you have in your life, the little things and the big things, and realise that you are truly blessed with who you are and what you have.

Exercise

Keep a gratitude journal for a week, or better still, make it a new daily habit. The more specific you can be with your journal entries, the better. So rather than writing 'I am grateful for my job', you might write 'I love the fact that I have so much freedom from my boss in how I get my job done', or 'I am so grateful for all the fun people at work, especially Freddy who always makes me laugh'. Make your entries specific to what you have experienced throughout the day, like 'Thank you Sarah for your encouraging smile today during my presentation to senior management'. And to give your journal extra power, make sure you share as much of it with others as possible, particularly when you write about specific people like Freddy and Sarah above – not only will it be uplifting for them to hear your positive feedback, it will make you feel even better, too!

> **Bonus opportunity**
>
> If you'd like to go the extra mile on this exercise and reap even more rewards, set aside a full hour the first time you write in the gratitude journal. Force yourself to write for the entire hour. I promise you, it will give you a whole new perspective on all the things there are to appreciate in your life. The last fifteen minutes of the hour are likely to feel excruciating, but I bet you will be surprised by what you come up with and feel great for persevering. After the initial hour of journalling, continue on the following days with adding new things, or different aspects of the same things, to your list for a few minutes each day. Read through your list at the end of the week, and allow yourself to be blown away by all the things you have in your life that you can be grateful for – an instant happiness booster!

How to get into a mode of appreciation

When appreciation seems difficult because things are not going the way you would like them to, remind yourself that the Universe is on your side, even if it doesn't look like it. The life lessons it holds for you are exactly what you asked for before you came into this world, to grow into who you wanted to become. If you were able to step away and take a bird's eye view on some of the little and big struggles you are faced with at the moment, it would be much easier to see the perfection of everything, and the insignificance of some of the battles you are currently fighting. If you're in the middle of something difficult right now, try to trust the universal process, write in your gratitude journal every day, and things will start to shift for the better in no time – the Law of Attraction demands it!

But, admittedly, it's not easy to be in a constant place of appreciation. Every day millions of internet users ask Google some of life's most difficult questions, and one of them is 'Why don't I appreciate what I have?' Yes, why don't we? Of course, we all have good days and bad days, so none of us feel like singing the praises of everything good in our life all the time. But what is it that stops us from feeling more grateful on a daily basis? Let's take a look at the biggest obstacles that might keep you from feeling appreciation:

- **Taking things for granted.** This is possibly the biggest reason we stop appreciating what we have. It's called 'habituation': we are so used to having what we've got, that we get desensitised to the experience of having it. Health is a classic example: if you are wired like most people, you naturally assume it's a given to feel good and be healthy, until you are struck by an illness. The same probably applies to other key things in life, like family, your talents, your job, your good fortune, and your possessions. By taking things for granted you miss out on feeling true joy for what you have until it's too late. Stop assuming you have tomorrow, and appreciate what you have, today! Pick up the phone and tell someone you deeply care about how important they are to you – because you might not get a chance to do so tomorrow.

- **Longing for what you don't have.** Another big obstacle to feeling grateful is when you are too focused on what you want instead of what you have. To find out how much this might apply to you, just listen to your inner dialogue for a day. Is it focused on all the amazing things you have in your life, or the few – seemingly even more amazing – things you don't yet have? For most people, it will be the latter. Start to notice when you are focusing on what you want but don't yet have, and shift your attention instead to all the many things there are to appreciate in your life. As per the Law of Attraction, the more you appreciate what you have, the more there will be to appreciate. If you would like some more help with this, take another look at the 'Law of Attraction' chapter in Part 1 of the book.

- **Being impatient.** Impatience is the third and final culprit I want to mention here. Impatience, by definition, means that you are unhappy with the situation as it is, and want it to be a different way. But not only that; even if things are changing for the better, the pace at which things are changing is not fast enough for your liking. It's not possible to truly appreciate something if you are experiencing impatience at the same time. I will talk about patience – and the power of it – in some more detail later in the chapter.

Which one of these main 'appreciation killers' do you experience the most? They are all quite challenging to deal with, but I hope that the following two simple techniques will help to counteract the above and bring more appreciation into your life:

- **Learn to savour each experience.** Do you enjoy wine tasting? When you sample an expensive wine, all senses get involved. You might start by studying the wine's colour and how it runs down the glass, before smelling its rich bouquet of different flavours. Then you take a first sip, and let the rich liquid run over the different parts of your tongue and throat so that your taste buds can fully appreciate the delicacy of the precious liquid. Savouring means taking your time, to consciously linger and fully enjoy each moment of an experience. Learn to slow down your busy life and take your time, as often as you can. You can savour experiences in the here and now, but you can equally linger and enjoy a lovely memory from the past, or savour the excitement of an event coming up in the near future.

- **Be thankful for the little things.** Being thankful for the little things is just as important, if not more so, than appreciating the big things. It teaches very powerfully that there is always, <u>always</u>, something that can be appreciated even in the most difficult situations. Even the most annoying person has qualities to appreciate; you just have to train your eye to look for it and focus on the positive rather than the negative. Remember: the more you focus on what there is to appreciate, the more there will be to appreciate!

Exercise

Being aware of all there is to appreciate is key to feeling grateful. Today, focus your attention on one thing you probably don't spend much time thinking about normally, because you're likely to take it for granted like everyone else who has it: your eyesight. When was the last time you consciously savoured your eyesight, and all the impressions it provides you with? Look around often throughout the day today, and just realise what a gift it is to see all the colours and beauty around you. Close your eyes, and consider what it would be like to not be able to see anymore. You will get a whole new sense of appreciation for the miracle of your eyes. Notice how they are able to capture your surroundings for you in all the richness of brilliant colours, shapes and movements. I promise you, this exercise is bound to make you feel good and buzzing with appreciation. And if you enjoy the exercise, you can repeat it tomorrow by focusing on the miracle of your legs, hands, nose or ears – the choice is yours!

> **Note:** The purpose of this exercise is to make you feel good by appreciating things you normally take for granted and don't spend much time thinking about. Occasionally, the exercise causes some people to feel sad or guilty because it reminds them of someone who doesn't have their eyesight any longer, or all the other sad things that are happening in the world. If this happens to you, then I suggest you pick something else to focus on to bring yourself back to good-feeling thoughts of appreciation. Feeling bad for someone else means you won't get the benefit from this exercise, and it won't make the situation better for anyone.

Appreciation and the Law of Attraction

I have mentioned the Law of Attraction several times already throughout this chapter, but it is worth revisiting it in some more detail now. Let's remind ourselves of the three steps to bringing what you want into your life, as mentioned in Part 1 of the book:

Step 1: Be clear about what you want
Step 2: The Universe hears what you want and responds to it
Step 3: Allow the Universe to get it to you

Step 3, 'Allow the Universe to get it to you', is where appreciation plays a quintessential role. Abraham calls it the 'Art of Allowing'.[23] It means being truly happy with what you have, and being excited about what will come into your life, <u>before</u> it actually comes into your life. It's about learning to trust the universal process, and letting things happen in their own way and in their own time, without becoming impatient and trying to rush things along. It is called an art because it is in our nature to try to be in control, and to want it 'right now'. Learn to let go of any lingering doubts and resistance. Trust the process and eliminate any 'but's' that keep you from aligning with the Universe. If your appreciation of something gives you goosebumps out of sheer excitement and joy, it is your body's way of telling you that you are fully aligned with the universal process, and more things to appreciate are on their way to you.

And here is the key: the more excited you are about all the blessings in your life, the more you are in a state of allowing and bringing more of what you want into your life. Doesn't sound like a punchline? Read it again. Because this simple sentence can make all the difference in your life going forward. Let me explain: if you don't feel particularly enthusiastic right now about all the things you have in your life, it is a direct indicator that you are currently keeping the things you desire away from you. It's not the Universe not giving them to you – they are already right on your doorstep – it's you who is putting a foot against the door to stop them from coming in. The good news is, you have the power to change this at any time: just get fully present to everything there is to appreciate in your life, feel the buzz, and get your foot out of the way!

The power of patience

Patience is a very close companion to appreciation, and if I had to summarise the 'Art of Allowing' in just a few words, it would be trust, appreciation, and patience. Trust in the universal process, appreciate what you have, and be patient to allow things to happen at their own pace. Patience is knowing that all is well, exactly as it is meant to be, and what you want is on its way. Being patient is not about being resigned – it's accepting and seeing the positive in what is, while being excited about what's coming. It's having an internal knowing that everything you are looking for is certain to come. However, patience is not as passive as it might sound. In fact, I personally think that practising patience is a difficult balancing act. How do you know when to let things take their course, and when to take action? It's a fine line between deliberate non-action and giving up, and while it might look the same from an observer's perspective, only you will know what side of the line you are standing on. If you are feeling calm and experience positive expectation in your non-action, you have found the right balance.

Every now and then, there are opportunities that pop up out of the blue, and only if you are ready for them and expect the unexpected will you be able to take advantage or even notice them. Patience is about being prepared for any opportunities when they arise, and expecting them. At the same time, you shouldn't get hung up about it if you miss a seemingly great opportunity. Other opportunities are waiting for you around the corner – when one door closes, another always opens! That's another key attribute of practising patience, to not get obsessed with any particular idea, and instead allow the Universe to come up with something even more spectacular than you ever thought possible.

Patience also plays a key role in speeding up the process of learning your life lessons, and resolving difficult situations. How so? Every seemingly negative event holds a lesson for you to learn, and if you refuse to learn it, it will repeat itself in different guises again and again, to teach you what you need to learn. If you can stand in a place of patience and calmness, and see the event as a stepping stone to your dreams rather than an obstacle, you are bound to learn the lesson a lot quicker. And as soon as you have learned the lesson, you won't experience these negative circumstances any longer. So even though it often feels frustratingly slow to not interfere and be patient instead, it actually often speeds things up in the long run!

Closing note

It is easy to take things for granted. I should know, because I certainly took my long, healthy hair for granted until it started to fall out by the bucketload a few years ago. The three independent specialist dermatologists that I consulted diagnosed it as a potential case of LPP (*lichen planopilaris*), but could never fully confirm this. However, they were all in agreement and in no doubt that whatever the illness was, it was causing severe permanent, non-regenerative hair loss (scarring alopecia). In other words, my hair would never grow back again. I was devastated. Eighteen months later, after various unsuccessful treatments by dermatologist experts, the bald area on my head had nearly grown to the size of my hand, and I was terrified. I had no idea until then how important my hair had been to me. It had become impossible to hide the baldness any longer from the public eye, and I was convinced that everyone kept staring at my balding head. It knocked my confidence and I became incredibly self-conscious. It seemed inevitable that I would have to wear a wig for the rest of my life.

But I am a very stubborn person by nature, and decided to start looking for alternative healing options. I had seen and experienced quite a few things already over the years, including Qigong to improve the body's energy flow, and Kinesiology to tune in with the body and identify any nutritional shortages or emotional blockages. In the end, though, it was a Chinese acupuncturist in southwest London (Caroline Cai, www.contemporarychinesetherapy.com) with her herbs and special form of acupuncture treatment that managed to stop the progression of the illness and start the regrowth of my hair. That was four years ago. Against all odds and against all the specialists' opinions, my hair grew back almost completely within a year, and is now back to its healthy fullness. I never had to wear a wig, and haven't had any further hair loss since. Needless to say, I am incredibly grateful for the miraculous recovery, and I have been treasuring and appreciating my hair ever since that very scary experience.

But here is the big question: is that really what it takes, some profound negative experience, to make us appreciate what we've got? I certainly hope not. So don't be one of those who ends up saying "I wish I had appreciated more what I had, but now he/she/it is gone and it's too late." Stop taking things for granted, and start to truly see how much there is to be grateful for in your life. It's worth remembering that your life, and every moment of it, is unique and will never happen again in the same way. It is a precious gift worth celebrating every day of the year, not just on your birthday. Don't waste your life on unimportant things; instead, make the most of every day and appreciate each moment as if it was your last. Appreciating what you have might take a bit of effort to keep up, but just remember how happy it will make you feel when you keep reminding yourself every day of all the amazing things and gorgeous people you have in your life!

AND NOW: OVER TO YOU!

You are joy, looking for a way to express. It's not just that your purpose is joy, it is that you are joy. You are love and joy and freedom and clarity expressing. Energy-frolicking and eager. That's who you are.

Let your dominant intent be to feel good which means be playful, have fun, laugh often, look for reasons to appreciate and practice the art of appreciation. And as you practice it, the Universe, who has been watching you practice, will give you constant opportunities to express it. So that your life just gets better and better and better.

Abraham (channelled by Esther Hicks)[24]

Choose your focus

This is it. You now have all the key insights and tools to create happiness in your life, day by day. This is the end of the book, but just the beginning of your exciting personal journey to a happier life. The question is, how are you going to translate and integrate the knowledge gained from this book into your life?

I hope you've had a chance to apply each one of the 10 Secrets for at least a day to see what difference they can make to your happiness and your life. If you haven't done so yet, spend some time over the next few days testing for yourself which secrets are the most impactful for you. Then it's time to choose. Which one of the 10 Secrets would make the biggest difference in your life in terms of your happiness and how you feel, if you were focusing on it every day? Personal change is most successful when focused on one thing at a time – trying to change more than three things at once increases the chances of failure manifold. With this in mind, choosing the one or two secrets that will make the biggest difference to you is definitely the most effective and powerful approach.

Starting the journey

Once you have chosen your focus, think about what you need to do in order to make the changes part of your daily routine. Are there any new habits you want to embed in your life? It takes about twenty-one days to introduce a new habit into your life, and I won't lie to you – the first few weeks can be tough, and it takes discipline to stick with it. So make sure you are absolutely clear about what changes are needed: what one or two new habits will make the biggest difference, and set the best foundations for a life you love?

It's helpful to illustrate this with an example. Let's say of all the secrets in this book, Secret 8 'Simplify your life' was the one that spoke to you the most, the one that got you truly excited. You experimented with several ideas in the chapter, and it felt like a heavy weight of mental and physical clutter was taken off your shoulders as a result. You'd now like to recreate that feeling on a more permanent basis, and get rid of more unnecessary burdens and complexity in your life. Of all the ideas presented in the chapter, you decide to commit to the following three things:

1. To declutter your home
2. To not watch any TV for a week (and maybe longer)
3. To start meditating for fifteen minutes every morning

You set aside a weekend to declutter your wardrobe and the rest of your home, and you feel fantastic once it's done. Both you and your home feel so much lighter and more joyful with all that old energy and 'stuff' gone! You then tackle your second challenge of not watching TV, and realise how nice it is to spend the evenings just relaxing with a book or listening to some music. After a whole week of not watching TV, you decide that you don't want to go without TV entirely, but that you'd like to introduce two TV-free evenings a week, and you put those into your calendar like a date.

The third commitment is the most challenging one for you, because it means you have to get up fifteen minutes earlier every day to make the time to meditate, and you are already struggling quite a bit getting up in the morning. You're worried about whether you will have the necessary discipline to stick to it. You know that you will feel great if you do it, because you tried it out while reading the chapter. To set yourself up for success, you decide to embed it as a new habit. You pick the time that works best for you to meditate, which is after taking a shower when you are fully awake. You decide that you'd like to meditate on a straight chair (to make sure you don't fall asleep), and you set up your phone with a gentle alarm to alert you when the fifteen minutes are up. If you live with family or a flatmate, you tell them that this is what you are planning to do, and you ask them to support you in sticking to it every day for the next twenty-one days without exception, including Saturdays and Sundays. This way you ensure that there are no disruptions, and by sharing your intentions with other people in your life it becomes a more official commitment, too. You have now set yourself up for success.

The above is just an example of what it could look like to choose your priorities and make them happen. One-off tasks like items one and two above are usually a lot easier to do than introducing a new habit such as daily meditation. Sticking to a new routine every single day will require a lot of discipline, but it's well worth persevering. After three weeks you should review your new routine, and make adjustments if necessary to make it work even better for you going forward. And hopefully by then it will be embedded enough to be a new habit that you don't have to think much about anymore.

Depending on what you choose to take on, you might want to consider using a buddy system, which can work very well: find someone who is looking to introduce a new habit as well (it helps if they've read this book, but it's not a must), and then schedule a ten-minute call every day for those first twenty-one days, ideally at the same time each day. Use the call to share your successes as well as your challenges and frustrations. Then do a weekly call for a few more weeks once you have both successfully completed the first three weeks, to continue to support each other in embedding the new habit. Buddy calls are a great way to ensure commitment and provide continuous mutual encouragement. They work very well to set you up for success on this important and exciting journey to living a happier life.

Give yourself a break

There is one very important thing that you need to be aware of when implementing your chosen secret(s), both during as well as after the first twenty-one days: despite all the knowledge from this book, there is no doubt that there will be the occasional off-day when you just want to stay in bed and not be bothered with anything, throw the duvet over your head and shut the world out. Sometimes we simply want and need to be miserable and feel sorry for ourselves. Because it's just not possible to be happy, positive and full of energy all the time!

For some people an off-day is just a minor dip that's hardly noticeable, and for others it might feel like a full-on depression – whatever it is like for you, be compassionate with yourself. Give yourself a break, and allow yourself to feel down for a while, until you're ready to pick yourself up again. Be grumpy if you have to be, and treat yourself to an extra bit of chocolate if it makes you feel better. Know that your lack of energy and enthusiasm in that moment is absolutely normal, and that things will look a lot brighter again tomorrow. If you embrace these 'down times', rather than fight them and beat yourself up about them, they will pass a lot quicker and feel a lot less painful. See it as the contrast that is needed to fully appreciate all the highs and happy times in your life. Try to tune in to yourself to see what you and your body need on an off-day to recover, and take it easy. Tomorrow is another day!

A word of caution: If you are caught by an off-day while in the middle of your first three weeks of introducing a new habit, I would highly recommend that you continue to stick to your new routine. Give yourself a break and take it easy with everything else, but stay firmly on course with your new habit. If you interrupt your routine at all during those first twenty-one days, it will be much harder to pick it up again the following day, and it will take significantly longer than three weeks to fully embed it as a new habit.

Live full out – your happiness depends on it!

After reading this book, I hope you agree with me that being happy is not rocket science, and was never meant to be difficult. After all, we didn't need anyone telling us when we were children how to be happy and have fun. It's time to start playing the game of life as it was designed to be played. Get the little hassles out of the way, deal with the bigger issues as shown in this book, then use the freed up space for what you came here to do – to be happy, have fun and live a life you love. Remind yourself that you are perfect exactly the way you are, and that you can become whoever you want to become. You are the author, movie director, producer and main character of your movie called life. It's time to stop being so serious about it all and have some fun!

I believe that we are here on this planet to experience three things: joy, freedom and growth. The essence of who you are is <u>joy</u>, so living a joyful life is your birthright. However, you have the <u>freedom</u> to choose what you want to experience and how, so you can choose to live a difficult life instead. Any experiences of grief, suffering and other forms of hardship all contribute towards your <u>growth</u>, and enable you to learn the life lessons you wanted to learn. All misery therefore has its merits, but wherever you are on your journey – I'm sure you have endured enough. So instead, with the help of the tips in this book, I suggest you use your freedom to choose joy as your new main priority!

Don't be one of those people who looks back at the end of their days, regretting that they have missed out on life because they worked too hard, worried too much, or didn't take any risks. Be brave – live a life true to yourself. You are very special, and you deserve a life filled with joy and happiness. It's time to make the most of this fabulous adventure called life!

Tips to stay in a positive mindset

I find it very helpful to have some supporting mechanisms in place in my life to stay in a positive mindset, an empowering frame of reference. Here are my personal favourites:

- **Subscribe to a daily positive feel-good email message.** There are many out there, and you don't want to clog up your email with too many messages, but it's very uplifting to receive a little feel-good message first thing in the morning. My personal favourite is 'Notes from the Universe' from www.tut.com by Mike Dooley. The website allows you to personalise the daily messages to your personal goals in a very clever way, and the messages are always very inspiring and thought provoking.

- **Surround yourself with positive, uplifting people.** It is hard to stay in a positive conversation and feel good if the people around you are being negative about everything. Avoid the gossipers and complainers in your life and at work, and make friends with people that have a positive vibe. You will know instantly which people from your network fall into which category, but you might not have thought much about it until now. I would encourage you to put your happiness first and avoid people that drag you down, and spend more time with those that lift your mood.

- **Set up daily positive reminders.** I find it a nice treat to put some personal feel-good messages or affirmations into the calendar of my phone at specific times of the day, say 10am and 3pm every day. It might say 'I love my life!' or 'I have such an interesting job!' When I'm in the middle of some work crisis and have that feel-good message appear on my screen, it helps me to put things back into perspective and get me out of any negative emotions.

- **Listen to feel-good tracks on the way to work.** I think there's nothing better than to start the day with some music tracks that make you feel good. One of the things that works particularly well to keep me in a positive space is to listen to uplifting messages from Abraham that are mixed with music.

There are numerous videos and audios available for free on the Abraham-Hicks website (www.abraham-hicks.com) or on YouTube – links to my favourite Abraham music tracks are on my Secrets to Happiness website. I have been listening to the same tracks for several years now and still find them uplifting every time I hear them.

Closing note

Writing this book has been a great adventure and a big learning process. It turns out that knowing the Secrets to Happiness, providing coaching and even writing a book about them doesn't mean that I am immune to days of grumpiness or exhaustion, just like anyone else. Becoming a mum while writing the book presented me with a whole new range of challenges, and I admit they got to me at times, particularly when I had to soothe our screaming baby daughter almost hourly at night, night after night for many weeks. It's easy to be happy during good times, but much harder during difficult times. I personally found that having a menu of options to choose from worked really well for me: on some days, nurturing my body, mind and soul with some ideas from Secret 9 worked best to get me back on track, while on other days it was all about applying Secret 1 'Choose what is' (such as embracing the reality of sleepless nights). Sometimes it was all about Secret 7 'Do it now', and other times I just needed to 'Get off it' (Secret 4) or remind myself of my purpose (Secret 5). In other words, all the secrets in the book found their merit while dealing with my daily challenges, and having access to such powerful tools made it easy to get back to feeling happy no matter what the circumstances.

There were times when I thought I'd found that 'end destination of permanent happiness' (I really thought I'd cracked it!), but lack of sleep and sheer exhaustion reminded me that there is no such thing as a permanent state of pure bliss. Happiness truly is a continuous journey and something that is created anew every day. Life will always present us with challenges. The secret of a happy person is to take these problems and challenges, and see them as exciting opportunities for growth, while sprinkling every experience with a good measure of light-heartedness and fun. I hope you have found inspiration in this book on all the many ways to experience happiness moment by moment, day after day. Now it's time to go out there and put it into practice – start living a life you love! And please keep me posted via my website (www.secrets-to-happiness.com), Facebook (www.facebook.com/the.secrets.to.happiness) or Twitter (@AlexWipf_Coach). I'd love to hear how you are getting on with your change journey and with using the 10 Secrets to Happiness. Happy exploring!

Twenty years from now you will be more disappointed by the things that you didn't do than by the ones you did do. So throw off the bowlines. Sail away from the safe harbor. Catch the trade winds in your sails. Explore. Dream. Discover.

Mark Twain (author, 1835–1910)

ACKNOWLEDGEMENTS

First and foremost, I would like to thank my partner and soulmate Paul, for his incredible support and patience over the last three years to help me make this book a reality. I would also like to thank my editor Louise Lubke Cuss and my friend Sandra Funk for all their feedback and support in making this book the best it can be. Furthermore, I don't want to miss the opportunity to say a big thank you to my parents for their unconditional love, and for raising me to become the positive and driven adult I am today – I couldn't have done it without you. And finally, I'd like to thank all the readers of my blog for their feedback and for spreading the word – because everyone deserves to be happy!

GLOSSARY

A Course in Miracles – A Course in Miracles (ACIM) is a self-study spiritual thought system, a course consisting of three books: a 669-page *Text*, a 488-page *Workbook for Students*, and a 92-page *Manual for Teachers*. The *Text* provides the theoretical background; the *Manual for Teachers* provides answers to some of the more likely questions a student might ask. But it's the *Workbook for Students* that brings it all to life, with 365 lessons – an exercise for each day of the year. This one-year training programme begins the process of changing the student's mind and perception. At the end of the year, the reader is left in the hands of his or her own internal teacher to guide all subsequent learning. A Course in Miracles teaches that the way to universal love and peace is by forgiving others; the course thus focuses on the healing of relationships. A Course in Miracles is a universal spiritual teaching, and not linked to any specific religion.[25]

Ho'oponopono – In simple terms, Ho'oponopono means 'to make right'. According to the ancient Hawaiians, 'errors' arise from thoughts tainted by painful memories from the past, which cause imbalance and disease. Ho'oponopono offers a way to release the energy of these painful thoughts, which provides healing. A key part of the modern version of Ho'oponopono (as taught by Dr. Ihaleakala Hew Len) is the three parts of the self, which exist in every molecule: the *Unihipili* (inner child/subconscious), the *Uhane* (mother/conscious), and the *Aumakua* (father/superconscious). When this 'inner family' is in alignment, a person is in rhythm with the divine, and life begins to flow. In other words, Ho'oponopono helps restore balance in the individual, and then in all of creation.[26]

Kabbalah – Kabbalah is an ancient wisdom that reveals how the universe and life work. On a literal level, the word Kabbalah means 'to receive' – it's the study of how to receive fulfilment in your life. Kabbalah is an ancient paradigm for living: five thousand years ago, a set of spiritual principles was communicated to humanity in a moment of divine revelation. This ancient wisdom unlocks life's mysteries and gives us the secret code that governs the universe. It's a system of logic that can alter the way you view your life. This extraordinary, powerful set of tools is known as *The Zohar* – the original instruction manual for life, the basis of kabbalistic wisdom. In recent years, millions of people all over the world have discovered Kabbalah and have changed their lives dramatically. Its timeless principles apply to everyone who seeks fulfilment, irrespective of their ethnicity, faith or religion.[27]

Kinesiology – The person that knows your body best is you. Kinesiology uses 'muscle-testing' as a tool, to unlock the answers to any question you may have about yourself. It helps to discover any subconscious sabotages that might stop you from having what you desire, and allows you to reprogramme those attitudes, so that you are free to make your life happen in a better way. It is often used to address health issues, using muscle-testing to identify nutritional deficiencies as well as subconscious sabotages. Kinesiology works through your inner consciousness, which is a key driver that keeps your body healthy (or not) and makes your life work (or not).[28]

Mantra – The word mantra can be broken down into two parts: 'man', which means mind, and 'tra', which means transport or vehicle. In other words, a mantra is an instrument of the mind – a word, short sentence or sound to help focus the mind. It is often used in meditation as a vehicle to help access heightened levels of awareness. Mantras are also popular to set intentions, for example while doing yoga: a mantra like 'I am in the flow' can help the practitioner maintain a clear focus regarding the desired experience while on the mat.[29]

Out-of-body experience – This refers to an experience in which a person seems to perceive the world from a location outside the physical body. For a brief moment, the soul exits the physical body and leaves it behind, attached by just a thin thread. It is most commonly associated with people having a near-death experience, but there are teachers offering techniques to having an out-of-body experience without putting the body in danger (**note by the author:** while I have attended some of these workshops, I have been unable to confirm their effectiveness – I haven't managed to have an out-of-body experience). While the phenomenon hasn't been scientifically proven as yet, there are many reports of people claiming that they saw and heard things (objects which were really there, events and conversations which really took place) which they could not have seen or heard from the actual positions of their bodies.[30]

Past life regression – Past life regression is a technique that uses hypnosis to recover memories of past lives. Past life memories are personal stories that explain who you are now and why you are here on Earth. A branch of hypnotherapy, past life regression therapy has grown over the last fifty years to be an important addition to the healing arts.[31] **Note by the author:** I tried past life regression simply out of curiosity. It was interesting to get an insight into one of my past lives, and it can be a useful technique to help with personal growth and healing. However, a word of caution: don't let your fascination with your past lives stop you from living this one!

Rebirthing – Rebirthing is a form of therapy which involves controlled breathing intended to simulate the trauma of being born. It brings into awareness not only your unconsciously held beliefs and emotions but also the relationship you have with your body, yourself, the people you are closest to, and your world. When you consciously breathe with this awareness, it becomes possible to resolve, integrate and heal previously unresolved issues within you. This frees up energy, brings greater aliveness and joy, and allows you to move towards fulfilment of your potential as a human being. Rebirthing is a powerful healing method which allows you to find true freedom in your life.[32]

FURTHER READING

If you enjoyed reading this book, then the below list of my top ten favourite books that have inspired me over the years might be of interest. Happy reading!

- *A Return to Love,* Marianne Williamson
- *Ask and It Is Given: Learning to Manifest Your Desires*, Esther and Jerry Hicks
- *Conversations with God, Book 1*, Neale Donald Walsch
- *Don't Sweat the Small Stuff... and It's All Small Stuff*, Richard Carlson
- *Manual of the Warrior of Light*, Paulo Coelho
- *The Four Agreements: A Practical Guide to Personal Freedom*, Don Miguel Ruiz
- *The Monk Who Sold His Ferrari*, Robin Sharma
- *The Power of Now: A Guide to Spiritual Enlightenment*, Eckhart Tolle
- *The Secret,* Rhonda Byrne
- *You Can Heal Your Life,* Louise L. Hay

REFERENCES AND SOURCES

[1] Copyrighted material, Esther Hicks, www.abraham-hicks.com
[2] Copyrighted material, Esther Hicks, www.abraham-hicks.com
[3] Copyrighted material, Esther Hicks, www.abraham-hicks.com
[4] Material excerpted from the book *Seeds of Greatness: Ten Best-Kept Secrets of Total Success*, Denis E. Waitley, Copyright © 1983 by Denis E. Waitley, Inc.
[5] Material excerpted from the book *The Power of Intention*, Dr. Wayne W. Dyer, Copyright © 2004, Hay House, Inc., Carlsbad, CA
[6] Source: www.wernererhard.com
[7] Material excerpted from the book *Conversations with God, Book 3* ©1997, 2012 by Neale Donald Walsch, used with permission from Hampton Roads Publishing c/o Red Wheel/Weiser, LLC Newburyport, MA www.redwheelweiser.com
[8] Material excerpted from the book *The Power of Now: A Guide to Spiritual Enlightenment*, © 1999, 2005 by Eckhart Tolle, used with permission from Namaste Publishing, www.namastepublishing.com
[9] Copyrighted material, Esther Hicks, www.abraham-hicks.com
[10] Material excerpted from the book *Conversations with God, Book 3* ©1997, 2012 by Neale Donald Walsch, used with permission from Hampton Roads Publishing c/o Red Wheel/Weiser, LLC Newburyport, MA www.redwheelweiser.com
[11] Material excerpted from the book *Conversations with God, Book 2* ©1997, 2012 by Neale Donald Walsch, used with permission from Hampton Roads Publishing c/o Red Wheel/Weiser, LLC Newburyport, MA www.redwheelweiser.com
[12] Copyrighted material © Mike Dooley, www.tut.com
[13] See www.landmarkworldwide.com for more details about the Landmark Forum
[14] Quote used with permission from Mark Manson, www.markmanson.net

[15] Source: www.imdb.com/title/tt0075148/trivia
[16] Copyrighted material, Esther Hicks, www.abraham-hicks.com
[17] Material excerpted from the book *Getting Things Done: The Art of Stress-free Productivity* © 2001 by David Allen
[18] Source: *2015 Global Emotions Report*, www.gallup.com
[19] Source: www.dictionary.com/browse/feng-shui
[20] Primary source: www.thescienceofeating.com
[21] *You Can Heal Your Life*, Louise Hay © 1999 by Louise Hay
[22] Source: National Qigong Association, www.nqa.org
[23] Copyrighted material, Esther Hicks, www.abraham-hicks.com
[24] Copyrighted material, Esther Hicks, www.abraham-hicks.com
[25] Source: A Course in Miracles (ACIM), www.acim.org
[26] Source: http://ho-oponopono-explained.com
[27] Source: www.kabbalah.com
[28] Source: Esther Kivi, Kinesiologist, www.estherkivi.com
[29] Source: www.chopra.com/articles/what-is-a-mantra
[30] Source: Out of Body Experience Research Foundation (OBERF), http://www.oberf.org
[31] Sources: https://en.wikipedia.org/wiki/Past_life_regression, http://www.carolbowman.com/past-life-regression
[32] Source: www.rebirthingbreathwork.co.uk

Made in the USA
Charleston, SC
11 January 2017